# COLLINS PO

# WORKING FROM HOME

### The Burton Morris Consultancy

**HarperCollins***Publishers*

HarperCollins*Publishers*
P.O. Box, Glasgow G4 0NB

First published 1996

Reprint 10 9 8 7 6 5 4 3 2 1 0

© 1996 The Burton Morris Consultancy

ISBN 0 00 472024 5

Editorial by S. Gill

Printed and bound in Great Britain by Caledonian International Book Manufacturing Ltd, Glasgow G64

# CONTENTS

# INTRODUCTION

Welcome.
In the early 1980s most working people went to a place of work, worked there and then returned home later. Home and work were in different places. Today, working habits are different – and they will continue to change. A book like this would not have been needed by many people 15 years ago. It is estimated that, by the year 2000, more than 5 million people in the UK will spend three or more days a week working from home. The shift in employment patterns is underpinned by the following facts.

- In 1995, 27 million people in the USA worked at least two days a week at home.
- In 1995, more than 1 in 5 people in the UK spent at least part of each week working from home.
- With organisations cutting staff and workloads spreading, more and more work is being done from home, often during evenings and weekends.
- Telecommunication links have improved dramatically in recent years. Teleworking is becoming an increasingly important feature in modern organisations, making use of video links, and the Internet.
- Self-employment has increased, among people who want to control their own work lives, and among people made redundant. Recent figures indicate that some 5 million people are self-employed in the UK, many working from home.

## The readers of this book

This book was written with four main sets of readers in mind – those who:

- would always have made the decision to work from home, running their own small business;
- are working for someone else, but are thinking of working for themselves;
- have been made redundant, or taken early retirement, and want to start their own enterprise;
- are employees expected to do at least some of their employers' work from home.

It is essentially a reference book, full of tips and information on what to do and how to do it. But it's also a book that asks some fundamental questions about the issues of working from home. You may find that your answers unearth potential problems of working from home. If this is the case, you need to come up with some strategies for overcoming the problems, or think hard about whether working from home is really a good idea. So it's a sort of 'green light /red light' book as well. However, if it helps you to discover that working from home is *not* for you, it could save you massive expense, stress and heartache later.

So you will find different sorts of material in the book. The material you would expect, such as:

- how to set up your work base at home;
- some of the legal and financial hurdles to clear;
- what it takes in terms of personality and individual skills;
- how to set up and plan your work.

But this is not intended to imply that there is a magic formula which guarantees success. Despite the approach that some books take – where they say that if you do X and Y it will all work out – life isn't that simple. You must take a long, hard look at yourself, your circumstances and your aims. This book also contains material to help with this.

Chapters 1, 2 and 4 are particularly relevant to people working from home as employees (or who may be doing so soon). For people who are self-employed (or thinking about it) all chapters are relevant. The nature of your work is, to an extent, not an issue. There is a very wide range of work that can be done from home. As the trends continue to change and evolve, the chances are that you will find a lot in this book that is relevant and useful.

Anyone deciding to work from home, either full-time, part-time, self-employed or employee should also link up with people who are already doing it. They will have a wealth of advice and ideas to give. But please don't forget to start at the beginning … by looking at yourself, and checking that the idea of working from home is right for you.

# 1  LOOK BEFORE YOU LEAP

## Why are you thinking of doing it?

Working from home is no longer a particularly unusual thing to do. It is becoming so much a part of mainstream working life that there are common factors and issues which can be looked at to help anyone thinking of taking this route.

What is clear – although it is impossible to pin down with statistics – is that the person who succeeds at working from home is someone who thinks it through, plans carefully and works out strategies for handling the major changes that this lifestyle brings. There are two main factors to consider:

- physical arrangements such as space, equipment, etc.;
- the personal qualities needed to make a go of it.

The first message is to stop and think before jumping in. Ask yourself some searching questions.

## What do you want out of it?

Consider whether your prime motivation is:

*Financial reward*
- the potential to earn more money;
- to earn just enough to get by, and pay the bills
- to cover school fees, to pay off a loan, or save money for retirement.

7

*Greater freedom*
- fewer or no organisational constraints;
- nobody to tell you what to do or to make you do work that you regard as unimportant;
- choosing when to work and how.

*Emotional reward*
- the excitement and exhilaration of being your own boss, with all the risks that involves;
- the chance to get away from a particularly awful boss;
- the sense of achievement that comes from going it alone.

Each individual has their own specific objectives. Working out what your objectives are is an important first step. If you know *why* you are doing something it is easier to remain committed.

## Why do people work from home?

Figures from the Department of Employment in 1993 show that in the UK some 625,000 people said they worked at or from home. About half a million of these people were self-employed. The others worked from home for another organisation as an employee. Other figures indicate that self-employment in the UK for the ten years up until the mid-1990s doubled to about four million.

These two sets of figures seem to contradict each other, but it should be remembered that not all people who are self-employed work from home. For example, many sub-contractors work away from home. These sub-contractors don't negotiate delivery dates or market the products they help to make, so often the only real difference between employed status and this sort of self-employed status is the tax arrangement.

For some people, working from home and running a business is the same thing. Starting a business is especially demanding. For this reason, issues relating to beginning a business are highlighted separately in this book, wherever it is appropriate. But working from home can mean other things too. There are increasing opportunities for employees of organisations to work from home. For these people, many of the issues related to working from home are the same as for self-employed people.

There are three main sets of circumstances that may result in you working from home under the employment of an organisation:

- you are offered the chance to work from home by your company. This is often seen as a perk and offered to more senior and technically minded people;
- you ask for permission to be allowed to work from home part of the time;
- you are required to work from home.

Clearly the third of these options is likely to be the least satisfactory. You may be confronted with this possibility as an alternative to losing your job.

Self-employed people tend to work from home because:

9

- they have always had an entrepreneurial streak, and decide to set up on their own in some way;
- increasingly, with organisations making staff redundant, many individuals decide to go self-employed rather than look for another job;
- there are ties at home, e.g. children, relatives needing care, etc.;
- they feel that their skills or talents are undervalued by their employer, and decide to go it alone.

## Early warnings

*If you are an employee*
If you are an employee, there are a number of reasons why you may work from home. In the 1990s many organisations began to realise the benefits of developing a more flexible workforce. Part of this culminated in organisations asking some of their employees to work from home, at least part of the time. The logic behind this is that if you ask staff to work from home it saves them the time, trouble and expense of commuting. It also saves the employer a lot of money in office overheads.

For any employees thinking of working from home it is important to be clear about the circumstances in which this is done, because these can have serious implications for the success of such a move. It is important to realise that you may need to do some negotiating with your employer about the terms and conditions of your working from home. There will be changes in your working pattern, and you will need to agree new employment terms with your employer. Just some of the areas you'll

need to consider are:
- what support from your company are you likely to need, e.g. communication links, equipment, etc.?
- will your company cover your expenses, e.g. phone bills?
- will there be any tax implications?
- will there be any implications for your income, e.g. loss of travel allowance, overtime rates?

There are a whole range of other issues, so it is important to think through all the implications of working from home and make a list of the things you should negotiate with your employer. That way, you are likely to reduce the risk of any problems later.

*If you are self-employed*
Working for yourself and running your own business requires a mixture of specialist skills and business management. You must have both or be able to develop the one that is lacking, pretty fast. Having business skills but not a specialist talent can work if you are running an enterprise that employs skilled workers. Equally, it is not enough to be a great cake decorator if you lack the business skills to stay on top of the accounts, the orders, the scheduling and the publicity work

Working from home is most often an individual undertaking. If the business grows to employ more than a single assistant, it tends to move from the home into specialist offices or industrial units.

You must examine all the financial implications of working for yourself, before you actually do it.

Working for yourself may not be right for you – **and there is absolutely no disgrace in coming to that decision.**

## What does self-employment mean?

At the time of writing, it seems as if the whole world is becoming self-employed. There are Government schemes like the Enterprise Allowance to encourage start-up businesses, most banks produce guides and give advice on small business management, and business-related courses abound. The enterprise culture suggests that 'anyone can do it'.

However, this is not universally the case. If working for yourself is more a last resort than a chosen pathway, consider very carefully whether it is the right option for you.

There is a real danger in the prevailing UK economic climate that people can be made to feel like some sort of failure if they don't want to run their own business or work for themselves. This is not only nonsense, it is unfair and potentially damaging. Consider the following, for example:

- not everyone is suited to working for themselves and it is much better to realise this before making a big mistake;
- if the UK economy consisted of only one or two-person businesses, there would be no large organisations to act as their clients or customers;
- if everyone were running their own business there

would be no-one to do the hands-on work that is the
foundation of many enterprises;
• not everyone wants the hassle of running a business.

If you are already pessimistic about aspects of working
for yourself, it is probably true that you were not
committed to the idea enough, anyway.

But don't be put off. Part of the purpose of this book is
to help you overcome surmountable difficulties by giving
you a useful advice and tips.

## Types of homeworking

### The business at home
Traditionally, there have always been businesses and
practices with a strong home base, where customers and
clients visit the practitioner. Examples include:
• dentists;
• GPs;
• other occupations allied to medicine, such as
physiotherapy, aromatherapy, acupuncture, chiropody;
• accountants.

Groups like these tend to have a dedicated room or suite
of rooms within or alongside the home, where they carry
out their professional work.

### The business outside
This group consists of self-employed workers in trades,
professions and occupations that operate from an office at

home, but mainly work at clients' or customers' premises, such as:
- plumbers;
- electricians;
- carpet fitters and cleaners;
- management consultants, health and safety workers, etc.;
- interior designers.

In these situations it is common for workers to keep equipment at home and set aside a space for keeping records, preparing quotations, handling telephone calls, etc.. A similar sort of arrangement often exists for the next group, where the home is effectively an office base.

## A home base
Many people use their home as a base for work they do elsewhere. Examples of these people include:
- sales representatives covering a territory;
- party plan and sales catalogue organisers and agents;
- service engineers covering a geographic territory;
- delivery drivers.

## Outworking
There are some specific points that are relevant to outworking.

Outworking is where an organisation, often a manufacturer, provides individuals at home with work to do, pays them on a piecework rate, and then collects and markets the finished products. The outworker is not an employee of the organisation, but is in fact a self-employed subcontractor of the organisation. Typical examples include:

- filling and addressing envelopes;
- sewing and/or knitting items;
- small assembly jobs for toys, cosmetics.

Outworking can be a very convenient way of earning money, but it can be problematic as well.

*The advantages of outworking*
When done for a sound and ethical organisation it offers:

- flexibility in when to work and where;
- the chance to earn money without the risk of setting up your own business;
- the opportunity to fit work around home commitments, such as children and other relatives.

*The pitfalls*
There have been many well-publicised cases where individuals have signed up as outworkers, only to be treated very badly, or even cheated. This has given the operation quite a bad name – unjustifiably in the case of the many responsible organisations that use outworkers.

If you know someone who already works as an outworker, and is familiar with the way things operate, they can act as a useful adviser on outworking.

However, responding to an small, enticing ad in the local newspaper can be fraught with danger, particularly as self-employed workers have fewer rights than employees. There are some important points to bear in mind if you are thinking of answering an advertisement.

*Responding to advertisements*

The first point is that it is often (but not always) the case that potential outworkers are fairly desperate to add to the family income. This puts outworkers at an immediate disadvantage, as they can be less discriminating about what they do and the guarantees they receive.

Second, be very wary of any advertisement or publicity material that:

- asks you to send money for more information, or a 'licence' to work;
- gives an idea of possible earnings – this will be based on the experience of someone who has been doing the work for years;
- contains strong messages about paying only for goods of acceptable quality, without specifying precisely what 'quality' means;
- doesn't tell you what the work is, but requires you to buy the materials or equipment in the first instance;
- starts to read like an advertisement for starting your own business rather than outworking – an advert might promise that if you buy the organisation's raw materials to make and sell finished products, you'll find people eagerly awaiting to buy them.

A simple test is to ask yourself a couple of straight questions:

- If the advert is the start of a working relationship that is going to be beneficial to you and profitable to them, why does their organisation want to collect a few pounds from you to begin with?
- If the opportunity is too good to miss, why doesn't the

organisation that placed the advertisement in the newspaper do it itself?

Even if the outworking is for a sound organisation, remember that:
- pay is likely to be pretty low;
- the income can be irregular, especially in areas of work that follow a seasonal pattern;
- the work will probably take a lot longer than you estimate;
- you may have to install equipment in your home or store quantities of materials;
- doing repetitive tasks, on your own, can be dull.

## What next?
Having asked yourself some fundamental questions about working from home, and given that your answers are encouraging, move on and look at your personal qualities.

## What does it take?
There are three key questions to explore here:
- what is it like working from home?
- what sort of person does it take?
- are you the right sort of person?

You need a positive answer to question 3, but you need to look at questions 1 and 2 first.

A useful approach is to use the recruitment process for a job as a model, with yourself as the interview candidate. If you have ever worked for a recruitment organisation,

you will know that the recruitment process involves three stages:
• analyse the job in detail – examine what anyone doing the job must achieve and what sort of environment they work in.
• specify the personal requirements needed to do the job – the qualifications, characteristics and skills – and separate them into 'essential', 'important' and 'preferred'.
• compare the applicants with the specification and select the best person, given that they meet *all* the essential criteria, and ideally many of the important and preferred ones as well.

## Question 1  What is it like working from home?

The first step is to analyse the job. There are advantages and disadvantages to working from home and what you should be looking at is the overall aims and context of the work. One person's pro can be another person's con, so what is a distinct plus to someone else may be a real minus for you.

*As an employee working from home*
An employee of a company will experience many of the pros and cons that apply to self-employed people. The problems caused by lack of privacy, isolation, and so on are just as likely. But there again so are many of the pros – the increased freedom, the reduction in commuting, etc.. What follows is a list of some of the particular pros and cons you may experience as an employee. You might

like to jot down other issues, depending on your own circumstances, the nature of the job you do, and the way you do your work.

| PRO | CON |
|---|---|
| **Status** Working from home is often given to people as a reward or perk. | **Resentment from others** People who are struggling to commute into work may be resentful of your 'perk'. |
| **Control of your time** Gives you time to think. It also allows you to be very productive, to see more of your family, and to organise the day to suit yourself. | **Insufficient respect for your time** Your personal space can be invaded. Strangers have your home phone number, and you may be deluged with calls about work at night |
| **Logistics** In theory, you can have everything you need in the one place. | **Logistics** Sometimes things you need may be at the office, when you are at home, or vice versa. |
| **Space** At home you can organise your workspace in the way that suits you. | **Space** Your house can become cluttered through lack of storage space. |

*As a self-employed person*
Working for yourself means that you must have the skills to do the work that your business demands. However, having a particular skill is not enough in itself: the successful self-employed homeworker needs the right personal qualities too.

*The context*
Working from home means that you have to handle the issues that arise from working alone, rather than with a group of other employees.

## The advantages
Some of the potential advantages of working from home if you're self-employed are similar to those for employees; others are different:

*You have flexibility in the hours you work*
- you may choose to work at night, early in the morning or at other times when you can work uninterrupted;
- you can work in blocks that fit in with domestic chores.

*You spend fewer hours travelling to and from work*
- you cut the cost of getting to and from work;
- you cut out the stress of modern commuting.

*Any income generated by the business is yours*
- there is a better chance of a direct relationship between the effort you put into your work and what you get out of it;
- you decide whether to invest in better equipment to

save more time, and to make the business more efficient.

*There is no boss to supervise you*
- you decide your own priorities;
- no-one dumps unexpected work on you;
- you have the satisfaction of knowing that good results are down to you.

*If you are a sole trader (page 63) you do not fall into the PAYE net*
- there is more flexibility in your tax and NI arrangements;
- large tax payments are deferred, giving you the chance to earn income before having to pay tax on it.

## The disadvantages

*Isolation*
- you tend to get fewer social calls;
- the calls you do get tend to be work related;
- there is no chance to brainstorm ideas with colleagues, to help find team solutions to difficult problems.

*Any failures are your failures*
- there is no-one else to blame and no-one else there to pat you on the shoulder and give you moral or emotional support.

*Success can bring its own pressures*
- if the business takes off, it may mean working

21

weekends, late nights, and bank holidays;
- annual holidays may become impossible, because you need to follow through work you have taken on;
- the anxiety of turning down work, because you are too busy, but at the same time worrying that you may regret it later.

*There is pressure when things are not going well*
- if the business is slow to take off, you need to work just as hard trying to kick-start it;
- to avoid panic when financial and other pressures start to bear down;
- to worry about dips in demand;
- nobody else cares if you stay in bed all day when you cannot get motivated.

*Social problems*
- it is easy to get so bound up in your work that it becomes your sole topic of conversation;
- it is easy to lose touch with friends and the social network outside work, by concentrating on your work.

*Physical difficulties arising from having a work space at home*
- if you work from home, there are fewer opportunities to get out of the house;
- friends drop in and distract you; they don't always see you as 'working';
- the privacy of what was the workplace during the day can disappear later in the day when other people come home;

- raw materials and supplies have to be stored or maintained in the home; this can be a real problem, if you need to take advantage of bulk discounts;
- unless there is room for a dedicated work space, you may need to get everything out in the morning and pack it away at night.

*Financial and reward worries*
- there is no security in lean times;
- the income you pay yourself has to be directly earned;
- you have to 'win' all the work you do; unlike in a larger organisation there are no dedicated sales or marketing people to win orders for you;
- some financial perks of employment, such as a pension, sick pay or subsidised travel, are no longer there – you have to organise and pay for these yourself.

*Having to wear 'different hats'*
- you do *everything*; you wear all the hats there are;
- there is no-one to give you support: no-one to do the accounts, send out the post, file reports, etc.;
- you have to spend some of your valuable time doing tasks you may dislike or that do not earn income.

*The risk of displacement activity*
Sometimes you will do anything rather than tackle the tasks you hate. Many accountants will tell you that the major problem with most businesses is avoiding the financial aspects. Many small-business owners prefer to tidy the office or check the work they have just done, rather than sort out a pile of invoices and cheque stubs.

*Learning when to stop working*

In most jobs, you leave your work behind at the workplace. Even if you spend many hours there, once you go home, you are away from the work environment. When you work from home, it takes much more self-discipline to close the door on work rather than 'just do a few more minutes'.

# Question 2  What sort of person does it take?

*Picture me*

Try the following exercise for finding out what sort of person can operate well, working from home.

Picture in your mind someone you know who either already works from home, or who you believe could do so successfully. Make a list of why you think they are or could be successful. Write down:

• the skills they have;
• their character and personality traits;
• any other factors that you think matter (e.g. physical condition)

Now picture someone you know who works from home and finds it really hard going, or someone you believe would not be very successful at it. Make a second, similar list for this person.

## What you found out

This analysis tends to throw up the same issues each time. They are listed below in no particular order of importance.

*Physical stamina*
- a seemingly endless supply of energy to cope with long and irregular hours;
- continuing good health to maintain the work output;
- concentration that does not lapse;
- sheer physical strength sometimes, if (say) there are deliveries to be made.

*Mental resilience*
- a consistently positive attitude (or the power to bounce back);
- a consistently pleasant and professional approach to customers, at any time of the day or night;
- the ability to handle awkward people and situations without losing your temper;
- the power to keep going when things go very differently from what was planned;
- belief in oneself and the products or service provided;
- an optimist;
- a sense of humour to help keep things in perspective;
- a high degree of motivation and self-starting.

*A vision and some clear goals*
Success comes from knowing what your target is. Having a target is much more than simply having a dream of where you want to be in life. If targets are not reached

failure will follow. There are three levels to this and each one should be achievable and realistic. What is needed is:

- a realistic and achievable vision of what life will be like generally, if your plans all fall into place;
- specific goals concerning your lifestyle and work;
- detailed objectives that make even clearer what is to be achieved.

*Planning and decision-making skills*

- all the decisions about developing a business and making it happen rest with you;
- 'jumping in' without thinking things through first is a recipe for disaster;
- it is important to base plans on realistic estimates and forecasts, taking potential pitfalls and problems into account.

*Determination and an action approach*

Planning and visioning skills are essential –so too is an action approach that follows the plans through.

*Support from family and friends*

Working from home inevitably has an impact on home life and/or close friends. You should have:

- a clear understanding with your partner and/or family about your work;
- moral, emotional and even physical support from the family and/or friends.

*The ability to do a range of things effectively and efficiently*
Effectiveness is getting things done to the required standards. Efficiency is getting them done without wasting time, resources or effort. Both elements are important and require someone who:
- can tackle all essential tasks, whether it is paperwork, cleaning up, selling, customer liaison, planning, etc.;
- recognises that all the business activities are necessary, and doesn't go into displacement mode rather than doing something unpalatable;
- is flexible, and can handle unexpected problems and difficulties;
- is not too proud to get stuck into things they didn't ordinarily do as an employee;
- unless you are organised across all areas of the business from the start you will never become organised enough to survive.

*A liking for people*
There is no work that can be done from home that doesn't involve people, whether they are customers, colleagues, family members, or suppliers. If you dislike people don't try to make a go of a business. It is other people who pay you money and cover your bills – and they won't do that for someone who clearly doesn't like them.

*Communication skills*
- the ability to listen effectively and *show* you are listening;
- skill in giving information and saying clearly what is to

happen, both face to face, in writing and on the telephone;
- a relaxed and confident telephone manner that inspires confidence;
- effective non-verbal communication, such as smiling, and maintaining appropriate eye contact.

*Commitment*
This is essential and includes commitment to:
- targets, plans and actions that have been decided on;
- the level of work required;
- promises made to customers; if you have said it will arrive on Friday, it must.

*Organisation*
Success in working from home depends largely on how well people can organise themselves. This area is looked at in detail in chapter 5, but includes:
- time management and the ability to prioritise;
- dedication to doing unpopular or difficult things;
- organising work-life so that there is time for socialising and relaxing.

## A superperson?

The above list of personal qualities needed to work from home is not exhaustive – you probably came up with a few other issues yourself. The list suggests that working from home is the sole preserve of exceptional individuals. However, anyone with *all* these characteristics and skills is unlikely to be reading this book. They will be relaxing in the south of France having made their millions. But there are thousands of mere mortals making a go of working from home.

There is every reason to try to aspire to the highest possible standards rather than trust to luck, but don't let this put you off. The point is that you should not give up unless you genuinely feel that you are not cut out for working from home. Many people have gaps in their make-up which they take steps to overcome, such as:

• review the skills and characteristics of a model homeworker;
• compare themselves with the model;
• take pride in the things they find they are good at;
• plan how to improve areas they are weak in.

This is your next step.

## Question 3  Are you the right sort of person?

To begin to answer this question you need to:

• think carefully about what sort of person would be good at working from home (page 24);
• identify your current strengths and weaknesses;
• glory in your strengths and concentrate on your weaknesses;
• plan some action to reduce your weaknesses.

*Analysis*
Rate yourself according to the criteria on page 30. The criteria are based on the issues raised on pages 25-28. It may be useful to ask a trusted friend to fill out the table honestly on your behalf.

| CRITERION | COMMENT | RATING OUT OF 9 | ACTION |
|---|---|---|---|
| Physical stamina | | | |
| Mental resilience | | | |
| A vision and some clear goals | | | |
| Planning and decision-making skills | | | |
| Determination and an action approach | | | |
| Support of family and friends | | | |
| Doing a variety of things effectively and efficiently | | | |
| A liking for people | | | |
| Communication skills | | | |

Make a copy of the table, and fill in the three boxes to the right of each criterion. In the first box – 'Comment' – jot down two or three words that sum you up in relation to the criterion being looked at.

In the next box, rate yourself out of 9; 1 is low, 9 is high. As a guide use the following:

6-9  varying degrees of better than satisfactory;
5    satisfactory but you may need to improve;
4    means that you need to take some sort of action;
3    is a bigger problem; and so on.

In each 'Action' box note down what you could do to raise any poor scores.

The first thing to do when you have completed the exercise is to take pride in the things you are already good at. This helps you to remain confident when you come to assess the areas where you are below par. **It is a common (and dangerous) trait in people to ignore or undervalue their inherent skills and attributes, while focusing on the weaknesses.**

You can find instances of people who are extraordinarily good at communicating, but they don't recognise it. To these individuals, communicating is something that doesn't need concentration. This is why a friend's opinion can be useful in spotting hidden talent.

So relish your strengths first. Then look at the weaknesses. There is always action that can be taken:

• studying a book;
• watching a training video;
• asking someone you admire for advice;
• observing the behaviour of 'role models'.

All this needs to be put into practice, so a planned sequence of skill development is needed. The best way to tackle this is to view skill development as a circle (Figure 1 on page 32).

This technique is simple, yet powerful – it is the approach taken by anyone who ever learnt to ride a bicycle. The concept is known as the learning circle. The learning circle works on the assumption that you are not going to try and change everything at once. Trying to improve on everything immediately doesn't work;

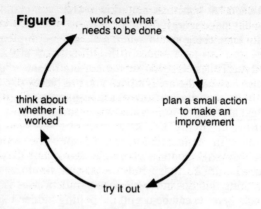

**Figure 1**

work out what
needs to be done

plan a small action
to make an
improvement

try it out

think about
whether it
worked

it takes too much effort and, when it fails, leaves you demoralised. Taking the decision to improve on things by 1% each day is much easier to plan and manage, and far more positive when it comes to the review period.

*If your self-analysis looks really bad*
If your analysis tells you that working from home is really not for you, then you have saved yourself a lot of further work, expense, heartache and disappointment. It takes a certain sort of person to make a go of working from home, and it really does pay to sort out at the start whether you are that sort of person.

# What are you going to do?

The next stage is to look at what to do when working in the home environment.

## If you are an employee

Employees need to think every bit as carefully about what they're going to do from home, as people who've decided to do it in a self-employed capacity.

No-one wants to have to go back to work and admit that working from home was a failure. The important thing is to plan carefully what parts of the job are suitable for homeworking, and when you should be doing them. It's a pretty simple process but you should take the time to work through it.

*Not everything fits*

First, it's important to realise that not all parts of your job are going to be suitable for doing from home. Indeed, you may find that none of your job is really suitable for the home. There are two major dangers facing an employee who has agreed to work from home:

• dumping;
• losing out in the 'politics' stake.

*Dumping*

You may find that some of the worst aspects of your job are dumped upon you, as you are quietly dismissed to the seclusion of your home. It is very important that you don't take home inappropriate parts of the job, or parts of the job that will cause you more time and trouble than if you were in the office.

33

*Politics*
People often disregard the politics of human relationships, but they are a crucial part of any workplace. Even though you may not like it, people do climb the political ladder at work, and a lot of this is done through face-to-face contact with other people.

All too often people who have been asked to work from home (even as a perk) have found out six months later that their job no longer exists, or that they have been marginalised. If you do decide to work from home, make sure that you leave plenty of time to network with people, attend meetings, and generally stay visible at work.

Frequently, the minute you become 'invisible' by working from home, people start to question how valuable an employee you were anyway. Especially, if certain people have 'points to score'.

## Doing the analysis

So it's time to think about what parts of the job you take home. There are two main elements here.

The first element is the job itself. You need to examine the job you do now and decide which parts you can do from home. The second element is your home. You need to analyse whether your home is suitable for you to work from, and identify any necessary modifications (Chapter 4 looks at this in detail). So let's work through the analysis ...

*List everything you do at work.*
Don't leave anything out. List *every* single component of your job, including:

- discussions with other members of staff;
- telephone calls;
- administration.

Draw up a chart of what your job actually entails to help you. Ask a colleague to run through the chart with you to make sure that you haven't forgotten anything. When you've checked your chart, put a cross by the elements you really must do at work, and a tick by those elements which you could do from home. Be brutally honest about this to avoid problems later.

*Unsuitable work for doing from home*
Essentially it is the 'people' parts of a job that are not suited to homeworking. There is no substitute for being able to sit down with people and discuss issues with them. You may find some of the following things are unsuitable for the home environment too:
- managing;
- team working;
- meeting with customers;
- negotiating.

Whereas the following tasks are all very suited to the home:
- writing reports;
- doing detailed drawings;
- reading or doing desk research;
- thinking;
- making routine phone calls.

*Work out the resources*
Make a second list of anything you will need to carry out the ticked items from home, including equipment and support services, e.g. more phone lines.

You should begin to see how your company can support you while you work from home. Avoid the trap that many homeworkers fall into where they are sent home to work, having to make do with inadequate facilities and equipment.

*Identify any barriers*
Draw up another list of any barriers that may make it difficult for you to work from home. For example:
- your home may be too small;
- people you share with may find it intrusive;
- you have young, noisy children.

We look at ways of overcoming some of these barriers in Chapter 4.

*Which parts of the day will you work?*
The final thing to think about is your work timetable. You may decide that it is best to work a number of full days to allow you to get stuck into the work you do. Alternatively, a series of mornings or afternoons might fit with your work patterns better, or your domestic life. It is useful to have a definite timetable if you are negotiating with a senior manager about working from home.

*Negotiate*
The purpose of thinking about how and when you will

work from home is to enable you to draw up a plan. Your plan should include costs, any time you will need to spend on the 'relocation', equipment you are likely to need, and details of the work you intend to do from home. You should also include a contingency plan to deal with any problems that may occur. It is sensible to suggest a review period too. You may well find that work colleagues don't understand what it means to work from home, and make unreasonable demands on you. You may also experience hostility from some of your colleagues who regard working from home as a perk.

You should take your plan to your manager, together with any other notes you have made, and agree *what* you will do from home, *when*, and with what level of support.

## If you are self-employed

When someone decides to go self-employed, often the only firm decision they make is to work from home. However, the nature of work to be done does need serious consideration. There are endless options.

## Deciding on a business

To help you with this, there are four Golden Rules, and one Silver Rule.

*Golden Rule 1*
**Never decide to start a business that requires skills or knowledge you don't have, or at least to a reasonable level.**

Given that the management side of the new business is probably going to be something you have to develop, you

really can't afford to be learning specific work-related skills as well. Remember, if someone is paying you money for goods or services, they expect to get:
- information on a range of possible options;
- advice on what is the right option for them;
- someone who is more experienced and knowledgeable on a subject than they are.

And you can satisfy these criteria only if you have experience in the relevant area.

*Golden Rule 2*
**Do not limit yourself to work you have done as jobs for other people previously.**
Many people, especially those with a lengthy track record of employment, have developed careers in areas that they have come to dislike or hate. It can be very restricting to swap employment for self-employment, but in the same work. Make the most of the change in work circumstance.

If you have little or no enthusiasm for the tasks you plan to undertake for a living, forget it. Find something else you have skills in. Otherwise you will find work tedious, and unfulfilling, and your motivation will be poor. Also, lack of interest conveys itself very clearly to potential customers. You may find you have skills and experience outside of your normal work which can provide you with an income from home. This leads us to Rule 3.

*Golden Rule 3*
**Love what you do, and do what you love.**

This is very similar to Rule 2. Make a list of all the things you:

• like doing and choose to spend time on;
• feel you know more about than most other people;
• currently pay others to do.

It doesn't matter what your list includes, it could be stamp collecting, dressmaking, antique china, cooking or following the money markets. The point is that in at least some of these things you may have specialist skills or knowledge.

You might be right in thinking that you can't make a living from (say) playing golf, but don't be too hasty in ruling it out. There may be options you have not explored, such as a mail order service for golf products?

You could end up rejecting all the options, but you owe it to yourself to give them some thought. The bottom line is that:

• if you spend any money on your interests, someone else is already making a living by supplying them to you;
• your enthusiasm for work in which you have an interest will convey itself to customers.

Naturally, any business must be run in a professional manner, and market research must show that there is a demand for what you have in mind (market research is covered in Chapter 2). But you would have to do these things for a job you hated ... so why not start with something you enjoy?

*Golden Rule 4*
**Do not be put off because someone else already does the work.**

If the founders of Compaq, Dell, Apricot and a host of other companies had decided not to make computers, just because IBM already did, the computer industry would be very different today. Compaq would not be one of the world's largest suppliers of personal computers.

The best place to open a shoe shop, it has been argued, is next door to another successful shoe shop. The mere fact that the shoe shop is successful is an indicator that there is a market for shoes in that particular location.

On the other hand, just because there is no shoe shop in your High Street, does not mean that one is needed. If it were, the big retail chains would almost certainly have opened one there already.

In business, you do not have to come up with something entirely new and different. Someone, somewhere has usually thought of it before. Inventions are the exception that prove the rule (page 50).

What sets successful businesses apart is that they do what they do better, in some way. Go to a guest house where they treat you like a nuisance, and you might start to think, 'I can do better than this'. A guesthouse is successful only if it attracts people back for subsequent visits, and guests tell their friends how good it is. The people running the business must:

• really like people;
• care about the quality of their guests' visit;
• be able to communicate with all sorts of people;
• be on top of the business side of things.

*The Silver Rule*
**Start small, if you can.**

The reason for making this a silver rule rather than a golden one, is that not everyone can start small.

Whenever possible, try to start the business part-time while you still have the security of another source of income. This 'double-life' is hard work, but spending a few hours a week developing a business in your spare time is virtually risk-free. It gives you:

• the chance to develop a track record;
• an opportunity to build up stock and set up systems;
• an awareness of what the market wants and does not want.

For example, if you want to open a second-hand record stall at markets and fairs, backed up by a mail order service, you could start by running a small ad in a newspaper or magazine, offering a list of records for sale with a request for people to sell unwanted records to you. You could handle enquiries during the evening, launching the market stall when you have enough stock and confidence.

For people who are unemployed and need to get their business established quickly, this approach may be unsuitable. However, one possible way forward is to do more than one thing at the same time, until one of them kicks off.

# A range of possibilities

Any business is essentially a process that adds some sort of 'value'. The business process has inputs which it

converts to outputs, adding something of value along the way. This point is illustrated by the simple example of manufacturing cake mix. The inputs are:
• the equipment – the actual processor;
• an operator and their knowledge of how to work the processor;
• space to operate the food processor;
• information (the recipe);
• electricity;
• raw materials, e.g. flour, eggs, milk and currants.
The process is the blending together of the raw materials.
The outputs include:
• a cake mixture, ready to bake;
• a processor that needs cleaning;
• an electricity bill.

Other examples are:
• a decorator who begins with paint, wallpaper, paste, skill, time, and tools, and converts them into a decorated room.
• a retail stationer who orders bulk supplies of A4 paper, paper clips and files, and sells them in smaller, more affordable quantities.

In each case the business has taken something and turned it into something more useful to the customer, by adding 'value'. This incidentally, is the basis for VAT (page 114).

There is an almost infinite number of potential business ideas and many books contain lists of these. Rather than repeat these lists, here are a range of broad groupings or categories of work. There are no hard-and-fast rules about which jobs fit where, and some fall into more than one category.

*Direct buying and selling*
As long as you buy cheap enough, you can make a profit from selling things (or services). You can:
- buy in bulk and sell in smaller quantities;
- buy a job lot of items at an auction, and sell them as individual items;
- buy a range of related items and specialise in what you sell, e.g. designer houseware, computer games, clothes;
- buy rare or unusual items in a speciality that you are expert in, such as antiques, records or books.

When buying and selling, there is a need to purchase stock initially. This is a good example of why starting small is important, as it can be a sound way of developing a 'nose' for what sells and what doesn't.

*Sales agency*
This differs from direct buying and selling in that you take orders, often from a catalogue, and the customer waits for delivery. Examples include:
- acting as an agent for a home shopping catalogue, cosmetics firm or household products company;
- party plan arrangements, which include perfume, jewellery, underwear, plastic containers and a host of other options;
- developing contractual arrangements with a range of manufacturers or suppliers, and acting as a self-employed sales representative for them.

*Lifestyle services*

Here you add value by doing a chore or solving a problem for customers. You could:

- walk pets, to solve the problem they have as a result of working during the day;
- provide an interior design service, to give them ideas and advice;
- operate a contract ironing service, to cut customers' workload down;
- take customers' shopping lists and visit the supermarket for them, to save them time and effort;
- provide house-sitting services while they are away on holiday, so they have peace of mind;
- visit their homes and provide hairdressing, a facial or a manicure;

The idea behind some of these businesses is that you can make a profit by being a specialist. For example:

- investing in specialist equipment – such as a large, commercial, steam flatbed ironing system – which will save you and the customer time and effort, while producing a more professional finish;
- in a shopping service, it is possible to buy from different stores at special discounts that are unavailable to the individual shopper, or to open an account with a cash-and-carry to obtain goods at a discount, so that the difference in price becomes your profit.

*Maintenance and property services*

These are fairly traditional trades but they do include some new ones. Householders and businesses will use specialists to do work them on their properties if they

lack the skills themselves:
- window cleaning;
- electrical work;
- plumbing;
- carpentry;
- painting and decorating;
- gardening;
- car maintenance and repairs;
- security (window locks, alarms etc.).

For the vast majority of these, trade training and experience – or at least a competent standard developed over time – are essential. So is an approved status, e.g. registered status as an electrical contractor or gas fitter.

*Health and social*
This includes some specialisms where professional training and qualifications are required (in the medical and paramedical field particularly) and others where any gifted amateur can make a start. Even where qualifications are optional, you are strongly urged to ensure that you pursue appropriate training and undergo examination wherever available. You are also likely to need professional indemnity insurance.
    Options include:
- the therapies: aromatherapy, physiotherapy, acupuncture, chiropractice, osteopathy, hypnotherapy, etc.;
- day care services at home for the ill and elderly;
- child care services.

*Editorial and written work*
There is a wide range of options here, most of which are very suited to working from home. Some examples of successful ventures are:
- copy and/or audio typing or word processing, e.g. theses, reports, manuscripts, etc.;
- writing articles, books, manuals and technical publications;
- copy editing and proofreading for publishers;
- translation and interpreting;
- desktop publishing and graphic design.

*Accounting*
Many small business owners hate doing the accounts but begrudge paying an accountant full fees for basic book-keeping and putting accounts in order, prior to a professional examination. For someone who doesn't mind this area of work, opportunities that may be worth pursuing are:
- maintaining accounting records for businesses on a computer, using one of many available software packages;
- manual book-keeping;
- organising VAT records;
- chasing debtors.

*Catering*
This type of work stretches across a broad spectrum, including:
- running sandwich rounds on industrial estates and in commercial premises;

- doing dinner parties;
- specialist food production, e.g. puddings, snacks and packaged meals;
- vegetable preparation for supply to other catering establishments;
- contract catering, for events run by clubs and other organisations.

It is crucial that anyone involved in catering and food processing of any kind complies with Food Hygiene Regulations (see Chapter 6). These cover, amongst other aspects, personal hygiene, storage and preparation techniques, and the physical environment (sinks, worktops, chopping boards, etc.). They are, quite rightly, stringently applied and overseen by Environmental Health Officers, to whom you must talk before setting up this type of business.

*Consulting*
This covers many specialist areas in which an organisation or individual may need to seek advice or knowledge, such as:
- management and business consultancy;
- health and safety;
- environmental management;
- planning and building regulations and appeals;
- food hygiene.

The prerequisite is that you are a relative expert and have considerable experience in the chosen field, so that that others are prepared to pay you for your advice.

However, the consultancy work need not be as a result of previous employment. Some of the most expert individuals in certain topics have become expert as a result of leisure interests and pursuits.

*Professions*
Qualified professionals often find it fairly straightforward to start a small practice from home. The list is very long, but includes:
• architects;
• accountants;
• structural engineers;
• landscape and garden designers;
• personnel, training and development professionals.

*Arts and Crafts*
Artists and craft makers do not always like being categorised together, so we apologise if it gives offence. The common theme is the creative process that involves producing or making unique items that are intended to enhance the environment of those who buy them. The items might be:
• a painting;
• a sculpture;
• pyrography;
• pottery and/or ceramics;
• a picture frame;
• furniture;
• specialist printing, paper making and/or book binding;
• crafts involving fabrics (e.g. weaving, appliqué, quilting, embroidery).

These require specialist equipment, and often serve specialist markets. If you are already involved in one of these areas, you will be aware of these.

*Manufacturing*
There is a grey area between what is manufacturing and what is 'art and craft', but the essential difference is the level of creativity involved. By manufacturing we mean areas such as:
- making items that appear one-off, but are actually based on a common set of components, e.g. designer wine glasses;
- assembling kits to make finished items, e.g. standard picture frames;
- making chess pieces and other resin-moulded items;
- mass production of items, e.g. pine cabinets;
- cushions and linen products produced in batches or runs.

*Other*
As with anything, there has to be an 'other' or 'miscellaneous' category. This includes anything that is hard to fit into any of the above categories. There are so many individual businesses that they cannot all be mentioned. A few examples are:
- fortune tellers;
- sports sponsorship and event organisers (parties, celebrations etc.);
- entertainment agencies and booking agents;
- recording studios;
- after-dinner speakers.

## Inventions

If you invent something which you are confident will change the way the world works, and could make you money in years to come, you need to take action to protect your invention.

First, and most important, *don't* take your invention to someone else and ask whether they are interested in making and marketing it. There is a strong possibility that the company will use your invention, if they think it is a good idea, and cut you out of the deal altogether. They could claim the invention is theirs, and it would be very hard and costly to prove otherwise in court. Before telling anybody about the invention, register a patent for it in your name.

### Patents

A patent protects your rights as the inventor and stops someone else pirating your idea. A patent basically gives the owner the right to seek legal redress against anyone who adopts the invention without coming to an agreement with the inventor, so it gives you the opportunity to visit potential backers and manufacturers, safe in the knowledge that they cannot copy or pirate your invention.

The ring-pull device on soft drink cans was patented, and nobody can use it without the permission of the inventor (who has become very secure financially as a result of a tiny royalty on each can made with a ring-pull). Cats' eyes in the middle of main roads, and the Black-and-Decker Workmate™ are also patented inventions.

To register a patent for an invention, you have to show that the invention:
- is new, and not known about or made anywhere else already;
- has a use – if it cannot be made or has no use it is simply impractical;
- goes beyond what someone else working in the field in question would see for themselves as obvious;
- is within the legal parameters; these exclude, e.g.:
- written and literary works, computer programs, videos or works of art (these are covered under separate intellectual property and copyright laws), although a new printing process could be patented;
- things that are illegal, pornographic, immoral or anti-social;
- surgical techniques (drugs are excluded).

You can register a UK patent with the Patent Office (the address for this is given in Chapter 6), or extend its scope for all EU countries. At the time of writing, it costs £25 to register a patent, £130 to pay for a search to check it is not a copy (even unwittingly) of an existing invention, and an annual fee ranging from £110-£450. The maximum life of a UK patent is 20 years.

Patent registration is potentially complex, so it is worth thinking about using a specialist Patent Agent to do the work for you. If you want to discuss general issues on patents and inventions, there is an Institute of Patentees and Inventors (address in Chapter 6).

51

You can also register designs and trade marks with the Patent Office and its sub-divisions (such as the Trade Marks Office).

# 2 WILL THE BUSINESS WORK?

There are several key questions that must be addressed to ascertain whether a business idea is going to be viable. The main issues looked at in this chapter are:
- finding out if there is a demand for your work;
- deciding if your business will generate enough income to make it worthwhile, and how to work out costs, prices and margins so that you can make that decision;
- deciding which sort of business entity you want to be;
- complying with laws and regulations concerning the home as a workplace;
- health and security.

In later chapters we will look at:
- raising finance, if you need it;
- tax arrangements;
- what could go wrong, and what happens if it does.

## Market research

### What is it?

Market research is a much misunderstood term. It is described by the Chartered Institute of Marketing along the lines of:

'...the management process of identifying, anticipating and satisfying customer requirements at a profit.'

In other words, a successful business does not emerge just because the people in it think that everybody wants

what it provides. The marketing of products and services is a customer-driven process, including:
- working out who your customers are;
- identifying what they want – often via the 'four Ps':
  *Product:* what are the detailed characteristics of the right product or service?
  *Price:* what are customers prepared to pay?
  *Promotion:* what is the best way to promote your product or service?
  *Place:* where and how should the product or service be available, e.g. by mail order, in a shop, etc.?
- using customer requirements to design your products and services on offer;
- telling customers about your business through appropriate promotion and advertising.

A lot of businesses seem to offer what they fancy providing, when it suits them and in a way that is easiest for them to deliver. However, increasingly, customers are becoming more discerning and quality conscious, and are more prepared to change suppliers.

Market research is not something you do only when you begin a business. Market research is the lifeblood of successful businesses, as it should constantly monitor what customers want, like, spend, etc.. Lose touch with your customers, and you will soon lose their business.

For many people, issues identified by market research are the cornerstone of their new business, and are used to seduce customers away from competitors.

# Doing market research

Market research involves finding out information that will help your business to be successful. If you intend to approach a bank for finance, the bank manager will want to see evidence of market research.

Large organisations often get specialist consultants to do their market research, but for most people market research is something they do themselves. This research may be less scientific, but any market research is better than none. The following sections provide some tips and hints to help make your market research as effective as possible.

*The aims of market research*

You should have some clear aims in mind, for your market research to be effective. Imagine your plan is to make pizzas at home and deliver them to customers. You would most likely need answers to these questions:

- does the market break down into segments: are there different groups of people who will buy your pizzas, e.g. local shops?
- how big are the market segments, e.g. how many take-away pizzas are sold locally each week?
- what do the market segments 'look' like – what are their specific and different requirements? Private individuals often want one thing, people going into shops another.
- when and where do local people buy pizzas? Are there high and low, seasonal or daily trends? Are successful, local pizza businesses in specific locations?
- will customers pay for a delivery service? How much?

- what is the most effective and efficient way of telling people about your pizza service?
- is it possible to make and deliver pizzas at a profit?

*Establishing demand*
This is the first issue that needs to be addressed, because it is vital to establish whether your business will attract any customers. If your research shows little or no demand for your work you should investigate other possibilities.

*Market segments*
Making a success of any business involves achieving sales that are as high as you can get them. It is easy to overlook whole groups of potential customers by focussing your attention on one group. Think about how many different market segments you can sell quality, hand-made table linen to:
- the general public;
- magazine readers – the general public who buy through mail order;
- local gift shops; ·
- up-market department stores;
- hotels, restaurants and cafés.

That's just five; there may be more. Some – like the first two – have strong similarities. Others have unique requirements. Each group is a market segment in its own right, because their *expectations* are different in each case:
- members of the public want quality table linen for their

own use. Quality is probably more important than cost.
- up-market department stores may regard exclusivity as the most important quality. They want the ability to buy in large quantities, and to have regular, guaranteed deliveries;
- smaller retail outlets may be less interested in quality. They may be more concerned with the price they have to pay you. They will want to place smaller orders that can be delivered quickly, so that stock levels can be kept to a minimum. Also, they will want to know if any product advertising and promotion is being run by the manufacturer which could lead people to the shop;
- restaurants, hotels and cafés also look for table linen that will last, and withstand hot washes and food stains.

All businesses have more than one market segment. Identifying market segments for your business just needs a little creative thought. The role of market research is to allow you to target each segment separately. You may need to find out different information for each segment, so you need to think about the questions you will ask for each.

Market research falls into two main categories:
- desk research, where you sit down and analyse information from other sources;
- field research, where you carry out face-to-face research yourself.

*Desk research*
Desk research generally involves studying published material. You might use desk research to find out the

overall size of a market and the potential share that could be open to you. For example, someone intending to offer bed-and-breakfast accommodation could check through information at local and national tourist boards, the local council and the library. This may reveal:
- the number of tourists visiting the area recently;
- the number of business people seeking accommodation in the area;
- the proportion of people that stayed in self-catering accommodation, hotels, and B&B establishments;
- how much income the tourist trade generated;
- where tourists tend to concentrate, and when;
- whether trends are changing, e.g. are visitor numbers rising or falling?

Competitors' advertisements and brochures are a useful source of information too. Desk research provides a useful backdrop to the more specific information that comes from field research.

*Field research*
Field research is much more pro-active than desk research, and can involve a range of approaches:
- observation;
- surveys, questionnaires and interviews.

Let's return to the pizza delivery service. You can find out background facts using desk research, but the only real way to find out how many people buy pizzas locally, is to either:
- stand outside pizza establishments and watch

(observation); or
- ask actual customers (surveys, interviews, etc.).

If there are no pizza establishments in the area, a survey of *potential* customers is important, e.g. would they buy ready-made pizzas, use a delivery service, etc.

*Identifying what really matters to customers*
There is a crucial factor in effective market research which has nothing to do with the products themselves, but about the expectations of customers.

If you are a customer with a choice of two pizza restaurants, and both have similar prices and facilities, which one do you choose? You should aim to find out what 'special factors' will make customers buy a pizza from you, rather than from the current restaurant they go to. This could mean looking at:
- how fast customers get served or have to wait;
- whether the surroundings are pleasant and clean;
- whether the staff smile and treat customers well.

*Structuring a market research survey*
Whether you ask people face-to-face, or ask them to complete a questionnaire, the questions are the same. However, bear in mind that the return rate for a postal questionnaire is very low – sometimes only 2 or 3%. Make sure that you ask enough people – less than 100 is probably too small. Generally, the more views you get the more reliable the results will be.

There will be basic things to find out, such as (taking the pizza example):

- do potential customers currently buy ready-to-eat pizzas?
- how often do they buy them?
- where from?
- what sorts of topping do they prefer?
- do they buy them from the same place all the time?
- how much do they pay?

There are also the 'softer', less tangible aspects, like:

- would you be prepared to pay extra to have pizza delivered?
- if you did use a delivery service, what would you want it to offer?

With this second set of questions, it is important not to ask loaded questions which force a particular answer. However, be prepared to provide prompts, if it is better than leaving a question unanswered. You might ask:

- In order of importance which of the following factors influence you when buying a pizza:
- the shop's location;
- the price;
- the range of pizzas;
- the quality of the food;
- the shop's opening hours;
- the customer service.

*Interpreting the results*
The benefit of asking the same questions each time is that it gives you a common set of answers to work on. So, if 70% of people said they would use a delivery service, it confirms that the basic business idea is reasonable.

If, however, only 10% said they would use such a service, you would need to re-think your plans.

**If the public tells you they do not want what you plan to offer them, listen to them and listen hard.** This may be disappointing, but it is better to find this out ahead of any serious financial investment.

*The competition*
When you have worked out what customers want, you must identify and analyse the competition in detail. Start by making a list of all your competitors. Split them into two distinct groups:
* direct competition –businesses doing the same as you;
* indirect competition – other places where customers could spend their money, e.g. take-away Chinese.

Identifying direct competitors is relatively easy. You can do this by:
* asking friends;
* looking in the Yellow Pages or local newspapers;
* walking about and looking.

What you are trying to identify is *the edge* that you have over the competition, so you can offer potential customers something that they appreciate is different. It is almost impossible to come up with a product or service that is *all* of the following:
* better than the competition;
* cheaper than the competition;
* easier to get hold of;
* better promoted and advertised.

Your task is to find at least one advantage that your business has over the rest, and it is likely to be in one of the 4Ps (page 54). In the case of a home delivery service for pizzas, the likelihood is that competitive advantage is in the 'place' category.

It might be that:

- your product or service is as good as everyone else's, but has a distinct price advantage;
- your promotion work is better, so you get to more potential customers than the opposition;
- your product or service costs the same as your competitors', but is of a better quality;
- your product or service costs more, but the quality is far superior.

What you are looking for is known as a 'Unique Selling Point' or USP. This is the special strength on which your business can be based, and is the hook on which you can hang your advertising and promotion work. Your USP sets you apart from the rest.

To find your USP – or to establish if you really do have one – try the following:

- list the strengths and weaknesses of your competitors;
- list your own strengths and weaknesses;
- compare the two lists and identify where they score, and where you do;
- concentrate on your strength(s), and see what you can do to make them even stronger.

Remember, if your products or services cost more, are no better, are no easier to obtain, and cannot be promoted more effectively than the competition, you will experience real problems getting started.

## Types of business

There are three main forms of businesses:

- sole trader;
- limited company;
- partnership.

There are also co-operatives, but this book does not explore this option. They are fairly rare and are subject to specific rules. If you want to find out more about co-operatives, there are some contact addresses listed in Chapter 6.

Please note that any information given in this chapter is for guidance only. Laws and tax regulations change fairly frequently, so check the current situation yourself, and always seek professional advice from your tax office or an accountant.

### Sole trader

Most new businesses start out as a sole tradership, even if they subsequently change to a limited company later in life. The term sole trader does not imply that you cannot employ other people. It simply means that in legal terms the owner or proprietor of the business is the same as the business itself (unlike a limited company which is an entity in its own right).

If your business will involve dealing with a number of large companies, contact them first to see how they feel about doing business with a sole trader, as some companies prefer to deal only with limited companies.

### Financial considerations

A sole trader is essentially the only beneficiary of any money the business makes. Equally, a sole trader is personally liable for any debts. There is no limit to the extent of any debts. So, if you run up debts of £10,000, you must find the money yourself.

A sole trader borrows money much like any other individual, and a bank, or other backer, will judge the sole trader much the same as they would anyone else seeking an overdraft or loan.

### Accounts

Naturally, any business needs to keep accounts. But there is no need for you to have your end-of-year accounts audited by an independent auditor. An audit is where a qualified individual scrutinises the accounts and certifies that they are accurate and above board, or raises questions if they have any difficulty in the certification process.

You make tax returns based on your accounts at the end of the year and you are allowed to do this yourself. There is no prescribed format in which the accounts have to be kept, and no legal requirement to have an accountant. However, bad accounting procedures can lead to confusion and Customs & Excise do sometimes carry out inspections if you are registered for VAT.

*Tax and National Insurance*
Taxation of businesses is complex and is dealt with in detail in Chapter 3.

In a nutshell, though, taxation of a business operated by a sole trader is subject to the rates that apply to individuals.

A sole trader pays tax in two lumps, bi-annually, based on the profit they make. There is no PAYE. While this means that the money normally deducted in tax can be used for the business, the tax has to be paid eventually. This can be a problem for some businesses, unless money is put aside to cover what can be quite sizeable tax bills. Personal allowances apply to the sole trader's whole income, as do any losses made in the business.

*The start-up procedure*
This is extremely simple. All you have to do is tell the Inland Revenue and the DSS that you are starting your own business – a couple of telephone calls will start you off in the right direction.

## Partnership

A partnership is effectively a variation of a sole tradership, so many details are the same. The difference is that you decide to work with one or more other people, as equals in the enterprise. Partnerships should be thought about very carefully, not least because even the best of friends can fall out over business decisions.

Working alongside others as equal partners in business is also a potentially demanding emotional experience. Trust, respect, and mutual support are needed, and this is

the case whether the partner you select is:
- active, and playing a full part in the running of the business; or
- sleeping – probably having put up financial support, while you work in the business day to day.

A key question to ask yourself is: how will I feel if the business is successful and instead of owning the whole business I own only part? Be honest with yourself when you answer this; it is better to face the question now than later when it becomes a real problem.

*Financial considerations*
Apart from the emotional issues of working with someone else, the main financial point to realise is that in partnerships the partners are 'jointly and severally liable' for the debts of an enterprise. This means that if the business runs into debt the partnership itself is liable. The partners can end up paying unequal amounts to settle debts.

Take this scenario. Two people start a business as partners. Partner A owns her own house (value £50,000) and a car (£6,000), and has £5,000 worth of savings in the bank. Partner B lives in rented accommodation, uses public transport and has £1,000 in the bank.

Through no fault of their own the partnership suddenly loses a large contract, because a customer goes into bankruptcy. The partnership is left owing suppliers £70,000 for materials, and they have no money coming in to cover it.

Partner B pays out all he has(£1,000) but A is liable for

as much of the remaining £69,000 as she can raise. She loses her house and car.

*The start-up procedures*

See a solicitor. It is always worth getting a detailed partnership agreement drawn up by a solicitor. Such an agreement *cannot limit the financial liability*, but it can specify, for example:

- basic details, such as when the partnership starts and whether it is for a set period – who the partners are and what the partnership is called;
- what the partnership is to do, and how it will do it – this helps to prevent one partner acting on impulse because they think they have a good idea;
- who is responsible and accountable for which activities, so that there is never any confusion about who was meant to do certain tasks, or any bad feeling about an unfair split in the workload;
- the arrangements for partners receiving payments;
- the hours, holidays and other 'employment' details;
- arrangements for winding-up the partnership, on retirement, death, ceasing to trade, or one of the partners simply wanting out.

A partnership agreement is never foolproof, but it does provide a basic set of rules, so that partners understand what is expected of them and their colleagues.

## Limited liability company

A limited company is a fundamentally different (more complex) arrangement from being a sole trader or partnership. A limited company exists as an *independent* legal entity, with shareholders and directors. You and a partner could own all the shares and be directors, but you work *for* the company as an employee. Employing yourself is essential, but it does mean that you have to arrange PAYE on the income you draw from the limited company.

*Financial considerations*
Limited liability means just that – the liability of a company is limited to the value of its shares. A company is owned by the shareholders so, if you form a company with £100 worth of shares and you own them all, the maximum amount you are liable for is theoretically £100. In theory, if the company goes bankrupt it is just bad luck for those who are owed money by the company.

In practice, if you are starting a limited company and want funding from a bank, they will not lend to you without adequate personal guarantees, backed up with collateral. Therefore the limited liability offered by a limited company is generally not as clear-cut as it may seem, and shareholders often have to put up personal savings and their home as guarantees.

*Accounts*
Unlike a sole trader, a limited company has to maintain detailed and extensive records of its accounts, in a form defined by company law. For example, a sole trader does not have to produce a balance sheet, but a limited company does.

Until recently, an official audit was mandatory for all

limited companies, although changes in legislation have removed this requirement for small companies (those with an income up to £90,000). Limited companies with an income between £90,001 and £350,000 no longer have to run an audit either, although they are required to produce what is called a 'compilation report' instead.

### Tax and National Insurance

As a company director you are legally a company employee. Therefore, the normal PAYE arrangements apply to you, with the company deducting tax and NI contributions from your salary. The company should also pay its own employer's NI contributions, and corporation tax on its profits (see Chapter 3).

### The start-up procedure

There are two types of limited company, both of which need to be registered with the Registrar of Companies. They are:

- a public limited company or PLC;
- a private company – any company that is not 'publicly' owned.

To start a public limited company (PLC) you will need at least £12,500 in cash, as the minimum share issue is £50,000, and at least 25% of each share must be paid for in cash. There must be at least two directors, plus a company secretary (who may be one of the directors).

A private company generally begins with £100 worth of shares. It needs only one director, but a single director cannot also act as company secretary.

69

There are two ways of setting up a limited company:
- form it from scratch;
- buy one 'off the shelf'.

Buying one 'off the shelf' is more simple, because someone else – typically a firm that sets up and sells limited companies – has done all the preparatory work, but the company has not traded. You buy the limited company, and initially trade under its existing name, at least until you change the name. The name change takes a few weeks and requires you to:
- pass a special resolution at a general (either annual or extraordinary) meeting of the company;
- submit a copy of that resolution with a small fee to the Registrar of Companies.

Setting up a limited company yourself is a longer process involving the submission of documents to the Registrar. A pack of these documents is available from Companies House (see Chapter 6) and contains, amongst other things, the following key forms and documents to be completed and submitted:
- Articles of Association – details of the rules and the structure the company will work to;
- Memorandum of Association – what the company is going to do, its name (which the Registrar will check to ensure it is not the same as, or too similar to, an existing, registered company) and its registered office;
- details of the directors, the company secretary and the address of the registered office.

There are certain things that a limited company's stationery must show – these are listed in the section on stationery, in Chapter 5.

## Legal checks on the home

One advantage of working from home is low overheads. There are no separate rent or electricity bills to pay. However, there are some potential barriers that you need to check up on before you start working from home.

*Deeds and covenants*

If you own your home outright you do not need to seek the permission of a mortgage company to work from home. However, there may be restrictive covenants or other stipulations in the deeds of the house.

So get them checked by a solicitor to find out if they contain any restrictions. There are instances where any sort of commercial undertaking is prohibited, but it is more likely that there is some specific caveat that limits what is possible, and lists what is not allowed.

For example, in homes that once belonged to a church or chapel, there are sometimes covenants that prohibit the sale of alcohol. To most businesses this does not matter, but it does if your plan is to open a restaurant in an ex-Wesleyan manse, or converted chapel!

In any event, check it out.

*Mortgages*

If you own a mortgage, you need to check your mortgage agreement. Some mortgage agreements do not allow businesses to operate from the property, as, amongst other things, this protects the mortgage company from losing income. Commercial mortgages generally operate at higher interest rates than their domestic counterparts, and have different tax arrangements. In some situations, the mortgage company may alter the terms of the mortgage if you work from home.

The simplest way to find out is to ask the mortgage company, as there are no clear-cut rules on what they will and will not allow. There is every chance that a mortgage company will agree to your working from home, but discuss it with them first, as in principle they could cancel your mortgage and repossess your home.

The main areas that might give a mortgage company cause for concern are:

- if you plan to make structural alterations to your home on account of your business;
- your work will be difficult to accommodate within your home without making changes to its purpose and use.

*Planning consent*

If your business means that you will have customers calling at the house, or you have to make structural alterations, you may need to apply for planning permission for change of use.

You do this by talking to your local planning authority, normally the local council. However, don't be alarmed by this. There are no hard-and-fast rules about planning permission, as every case is different and must be judged on its own merits. But you are likely to need planning permission if:

- your business means that your home is no longer principally a dwelling;
- you expect a significant increase in the number of cars, people, deliveries, etc. as a result of the business;
- your business means that you carry out activities that are not generally acceptable in a residential area;
- neighbours experience any annoyance.

You are advised to check *everything* that you are not sure of, as every case is different. The above guidelines are in no way definitive. Be mindful about any 'increase of user' or 'intensity of user', as these can also amount to 'change of use'. For example, you may be allowed to park one caravan in your garden without planning permission, but you could require planning consent to park two or more caravans.

*Neighbours*
Getting the neighbours on your side is a very positive first step if you need planning permission. The most common way for planning authorities to find out about possible problems is when neighbours telephone to complain. Even if you have received planning permission for your business, this does not prevent a neighbour from suing you, if you are causing a nuisance. There are two actions that you should take, with regard to your neighbours:

- empathise with them – put yourself in their shoes and imagine that it is them starting *your* business next door. Only in this way, can you begin to understand what their feelings and reactions might be. How would you

feel if you lived in a quiet street, and then the neighbours started repairing and servicing lorries on their driveway, or opened up a drumming school?
• talk to your neighbours about your plans. People get very upset if they feel that they have been ignored; and this makes them more likely to complain. Discussing things with your neighbours gives them the chance to express their fears (or their support, which is often readily given). Also, it gives you the chance to explain your plans properly, and iron out any false assumptions or misconceptions they may have.

## Health and safety

Health and safety are not issues only for large companies. Any business has to make sure it complies with health and safety regulations, including those run from home.

You are recommended to contact experts at the Health & Safety Executive (HSE) for advice and information (see Chapter 6). This is particularly important if you intend to manufacture things or use any materials or substances that could be harmful. They are there to help and can provide leaflets and booklets on virtually any health and safety topic, often free of charge. Trade associations also frequently offer help and information on trade-specific issues.

Life is much cheaper, easier and more productive if you prevent accidents and illnesses happening in the first place. A bad health and safety record is a black mark in customers' minds.

Remember: more accidents happen in the home than in

the workplace. **Pay special attention to health and safety in the home/work environment.**

The DTI Consumer Safety Unit publishes figures that show:

- 2.5 million people a year need medical treatment following an accident at home;
- 4,000 deaths a year result from accidents at home.

The more likely causes of accidents are slips and trips, but no matter how trivial an action seems, if it improves health and safety, **do it**. Avoiding an accident is ultimately preferable. Apart from suffering personal injury, an accident, may mean:

- loss of income, yet still having to pay bills, invoices;
- risk of losing contracts because you are out of action;
- loss of an opportunity to grow your business, because you are out of action, or you have to make good the work shortfall, instead of chasing new customers.

## Your responsibilities

Your first responsibility is to inform the appropriate authority that you are operating a business. This is likely to be the local council if you intend to run a non-manufacturing operation, such as:

- an office;
- a catering establishment such as a café or restaurant;
- a storage facility.

If you intend to run any other type of business notify the HSE. Remember that an HSE inspector has the right to enter your premises and carry out an inspection. They can issue notices of closure or demand improvements, if they find things that are not to their liking. Remember: you are the person likely to be harmed in an accident, and you will pay for any subsequent costs or fines.

## Other legal requirements

Common legal requirements that may be particularly relevant to working from home:

- if you employ five or more people, you must have a written health and safety policy and distribute it to all employees. The policy needs to make clear what the arrangements are for preventing accidents, and who is responsible for what;
- you have to carry out risk assessments, which we will look at in detail shortly, and if you employ five or more people, you must record your findings;
- you must display a current certificate of Employers' Liability Insurance, and the *Health & Safety Law* poster if you employ anyone;
- it is a requirement that the appropriate body is notified of any accidents and certain notifiable diseases;
- the regulations on Control of Substances Hazardous to Health (COSHH) must be complied with. This includes carrying out a risk assessment which is not restricted to just acids and toxic chemicals; it includes everyday substances found in virtually every business, such as correction fluid, cleaning materials and glues;
- special hygiene precautions are needed if food is handled or prepared;.
- users of visual display units (including yourself) must:
- be trained about the health and safety aspects;

– have regular eye tests;
– have sufficient breaks in activity.
• the place you work in must be in good repair and:
– have obstruction-free stairs, walkways, etc.;
– have windows that can be opened and cleaned easily;
– be well lit (with natural light wherever possible);
– be ventilated, heated and spacious;
– have handrails on stairs, and ramps where appropriate;
– contain facilities for disposing of waste and rubbish;
– provide adequate toilet, washing and drying facilities,
  and a supply of drinking water;
– comply with the appropriate fire regulations, in terms
  of fire doors, exits, extinguishers, etc. (the Fire Service
  rather than HSE advises on this, and in certain
  situations, e.g. guest houses, there are specific legal
  requirements under the Fire Precautions Act, 1971).
• any gas appliances in the workplace must be fitted,
  repaired and serviced by a qualified engineer.
• any manual handling of goods must be avoided where
  there is a risk of injury, and the risks should be assessed
  to minimise the chances of accident or injury.
• if you have any employees, you must determine safe
  systems of working and ensure that they are followed –
  you must also train people as required, so that they are
  aware of the health and safety risks.

## Changing the home environment

Working from home increases the amount of equipment,
materials and goods stored there. This changes the home
environment.

*Electrical safety*

Virtually all businesses use electrical equipment, ranging from computers to sewing machines to food mixers and lights. Your business activities might mean that your existing wiring and fuses need upgrading to cope with the extra load. Have an electrician check things out and do any remedial work needed.

*Structural safety*

If you are planning to convert an unused space in the house to a work area, you may need planning permission, and you will need building control approval for the technical specifications you will use for the conversion. These are not merely bureaucratic obstacles; they may stop your house falling down and taking the neighbour's house with it.

Call in an architect – having first confirmed that their initial visit is free. He or she will be in a position to advise you on planning matters, building regulations, loadings, insulation and other construction standards.

Alternatively, ask someone from the planning department of your local council to call in. Remember: council planners prefer to help members of the public to get things right, rather than mop up after a disaster.

Downstairs walls are often load-bearing, and knocking through a doorway could have disastrous consequences. Similarly, opening up the loft space by removing the occasional timber beam can lead to serious problems. If a loft space has never had to carry any weight and has a series of beams on its floor with plaster in between them, it is not the loft floor – it is the bedroom ceiling! Ceilings are not designed to take weights.

There should be no problem with putting heavier weights on ground floors, but beware that in older properties in particular, the use of an upstairs spare bedroom may need checking out. Imagine a fairly standard office and the equipment it may include:

- a desk and chair;
- furniture for visitors;
- a computer;
- a photocopier;
- telephone and fax machine;
- filing cabinets;
- maybe a small safe;
- books, bookshelves, files, samples;
- other paraphernalia, such as lamps.

In houses built several decades ago, the floor construction may be inadequate to carry a load like this safely. It may be fine for a bed, a few other pieces of furniture, and a couple of people, but the load from business equipment is much greater. Your floor may need strengthening.

*Special adaptations*
Many businesses run from home can be started quite simply and easily, with no special alterations or additions to the home. However, talk to an expert and get their advice.

For example, in a catering operation, an under-used oven and sink might seem ideal for making specialist dishes that can go out to dinner parties or cafes, but the Environmental Health Department of your local council should be consulted, as there are many Food Hygiene Regulations, including:

- separate sinks and basins for hand washing;
- working surfaces of a very high standard (stainless steel is ideal);
- clean and easy-to-clean floors;
- separate storage facilities for domestic and business food including refrigeration to set levels, and separation of various food items (e.g. no cooked meat alongside raw meat);
- chopping boards (generally high-grade special laminate, colour-coded boards; not wooden) and knives should be used for specific purposes only (e.g. one for cooked meat, one for vegetables etc.);
- a scrupulously high standard of cleanliness everywhere, which is a great deal higher than tolerated in most domestic kitchens.

All these are subject to inspection at later dates, and if the business has started without the right equipment, it can be closed down instantly. A basic hygiene certificate must be obtained too, which involves going on a short course and passing a written test.

*Who you are responsible for*
You are responsible for your own health and safety, but you are also responsible for the health and safety of:

- any employees, whether part-time, full-time, permanent, temporary or casual;
- anyone else working with you or visiting your premises, e.g. customers, contractors;

- anyone who may be affected by what you make or do; for example, you may use toxic materials whose fumes could drift into the street;
- anyone buying what you make or using what you provide – your customers and clients.

Putting up a notice disclaiming responsibility for any injury or illness does not work. You cannot shed legal responsibility merely by saying you intend to.

# Risk assessment

Assessing risk is a common-sense approach to preventing accidents and potential health problems. Risk assessment is a legal requirement of businesses and there are six stages in a typical risk assessment process.

*Stage 1  Identify the hazards*
Hazards are potential problems. In the home they include:
- trailing wires from machines, telephones or appliances;
- frayed or kinked carpet;
- slippery floors or rugs;
- storing heavy items on the first floor, so that raw materials and finished products have to be carried up and down stairs, unnecessarily;
- electric tools.

Walk around your home, and make a note of anything that could cause harm or damage.

*Stage 2   Decide who could be harmed, and how*
If something did go wrong, what would the effect be for
each potential hazard?
- who could be affected – not only the obvious people
  like yourself, but any others, like:
- any children who stray into the work area;
- neighbours;
- the cleaner, if you have one;
- any visitors;
- what degree of harm could the hazard cause – slight,
  potentially serious, serious, etc..

*Stage 3   Assess the risk*
The risk is not the same as the hazard. If you have a
frayed carpet that is tucked away under a desk, the risk of
it causing harm is minuscule. But if the fray is half-way
up a flight of stairs, the risk rises dramatically.
  Both the likelihood of a hazard causing an accident,
and the possible seriousness of its effect, need to be
considered when assessing risk. Ask yourself two
questions:
- how likely is it that something will go wrong?
- how great will the effect be if it does go wrong? (This
  second part is effectively the answer to stage 2.)

  A fairly likely occurrence that can cause a medium
level of harm could well be a greater risk than an unlikely
occurrence that would cause serious harm. There is no
magic formula for assessing risk.

*Stage 4  Review the precautions in place*

The bottom line here is whether the precautions you have put in place are adequate to control the level of risk. Try first to remove the risk altogether, but if that is not possible, do everything needed to control the level of risk.

There are no definitive rules for which precautions cover specific risks although there are many tips and hints in publications like:

• HSE leaflets – these have the benefit of experience from other people's misfortunes;
• manufacturers' instruction booklets and leaflets, e.g. they may suggest wearing protective goggles or gloves, or to avoid inhaling fumes, etc..
• articles in industry-wide journals and magazines.

The following two case studies serve as examples of risks and some appropriate precautions to take.

| HAZARD | PRECAUTIONS |
|--------|-------------|
| You use electric tools | Install residual circuit breakers. Lock the door of the room the tools are in when you are not there personally. |
| You lift heavy items | Avoid putting them on the floor, to reduce the amount of bending over, and minimise the distance you have to carry them. Practise sensible lifting techniques. Prevent anyone else trying to be helpful and lifting them for you. |

If you have done all you can to limit risks, you have done enough in the eyes of the law. If there is more that can be done... do it. The regulations say that you must do 'whatever is reasonably practicable'.

*Stage 5  Write it down*
This is a legal requirement only if you have five or more employees, but it is good practice to do it anyway. All you need to note down is something to demonstrate that you:
• did a proper check on hazards and risks (although you do not have to say how you did it);
• thought about who and how many people could be harmed, and in what way;
• confirmed that existing precautions were adequate, or that you took action to limit the risk where necessary.

*Stage 6  Do it again*
From time to time repeat your risk assessment. This is for two reasons:
• it is very easy to get so used to a hazard that you simply stop noticing it;
• things change – new machines, materials, circumstances, etc. – and old precautions may need updating.

# COSHH
The key requirements of The Control of Substances Hazardous to Health (COSHH) Regulations, (published 1988), are that:
• the six stages outlined above must be applied to any

substances that could be hazardous to health;
- appropriate training and information on the risks and how to control them must be provided;
- the exposure levels and health of people involved may need monitoring.

Basically, COSHH insists that a risk assessment is carried out for any substance that is potentially harmful to people. This is to prevent or reduce the extent of health problems such as lung and respiratory complaints, or skin disorders. Harmful substances may be contained in supplies brought into the business, or may result from business-related activities. The substances include:
- micro-organisms and bacteria;
- chemicals that are used, could be spilt, may leak;
- dust and particles;
- fumes and toxic substances.

Hazardous substances are often marked as such on their containers, with labels, symbols and other information. But you also need to consider:
- what you know from your own experience and common-sense about substances;
- asking trade associations and other people in the same business about what they know or have discovered;
- asking HSE for advice and guidance on which substances are considered dangerous in your business field, and the recommended precautions.

## First aid

Consider going on a first aid course. The local St John Ambulance, Red Cross or HSE will be able to give you information on where courses take place.

If you are working from home for an employer, it may be worth asking them if they will pay for you to go on one.

Buy (or get your employer to buy) a ready-assembled First Aid Kit, or make one up to the HSE recommended specification, which includes:

• 20 assorted sterile plasters;
• 6 safety pins;
• 2 sterile eye patches;
• 6 triangular bandages;
• unmedicated dressings – 6 medium sized, 2 large and 3 extra large;
• a First Aid instruction card or leaflet.

If you use any of the items, remember to top up the kit immediately. Note that the list excludes aspirin or any other medication. This is because such drugs could be inappropriate for some people with existing conditions, or who have recently taken other or similar drugs.

## Anticipating problems

At the planning stage, before you start working from home, it pays to think through some 'what if' scenarios.

Some of the likely issues to consider are: what if ...

• you are ill?
• there is a burglary and your equipment is stolen?
• your equipment/vehicle breaks down?

- there is a fire at home?
- you run over a customer's dog, or knock down a wall when parking on a customer's premises?
- a supplier lets you down?
- someone does not pay on time?
- your children/partner are ill?

Some of these points, and a multitude of others can be tackled only by each individual, in the light of their own circumstances. Others can be covered by insurance, maintenance or simple security measures. The important point is to make contingency plans. That way, you can formulate a clear approach for when something does happen.

## Precautions you can take

*Insurance*
You *must* inform your home insurance company that you will be working from home. This prevents the possibility that they refuse any future claims, because you failed to tell them of a 'material change in your circumstances'. Insurance cover you should or could consider is:

- health – permanent health insurance provides at least a basic income, if you are ill and cannot work;
- equipment and premises – on the lines of contents and buildings insurance; some companies now offer special combined policies that include working from home as part of a single policy together with domestic insurance;
- professional indemnity – covers advice or other

professional services you give that a client acts on;
- public liability (if it does not come automatically as part of other business insurance) – covers accidents and incidents involving anyone on your premises or yourself while you are out;
- vehicle – if you are going to use your car for business purposes, e.g. carrying light goods or people, extend your policy. If you have an accident when you are taking a client back to the train station, and you have only ordinary insurance, your insurance company may not pay up.

Talk to your insurance broker about the range of insurances that someone working from home could and should consider.

*Security and fire*
Increased security may be important, if you are working from home and will have extra equipment, stock or materials. Think about:
- upgrading the locks;
- installing or upgrading an alarm;
- putting in security lights with an infra-red trigger;
- making equipment more secure, by fitting special theft-prevention kits (e.g. inexpensive kits are available to secure a computer or other electronic equipment to a desk);
- installing or upgrading smoke alarms;
- having fire extinguishers to hand (obtainable from most office equipment suppliers).

*Information security*

Losing a machine may be a blow, but losing the information you need to keep a business running is a disaster. A computer can be replaced. but the information it holds can be priceless, e.g. unpaid invoices, contacts, etc. If you are going to use any sort of electronic data device, always:

- make regular back-up copies of your information onto separate disks or other storage media;
- keep the back-up copies in a totally different place from the original, ideally in a fireproof safe (available from most office supply companies).

Information on paper should be kept locked in a cabinet, preferably a fire-proof one.

*Alternative suppliers*

Wherever possible try to spread the risk of a supplier letting you down or going out of business. It is important to build relationships with suppliers, so they:

- know what you want and why;
- understand and take seriously your orders, the importance of deadlines, and any other requirements that you have;
- can offer you bulk discount;
- can offer credit terms when you need them.

Another downside of relying on a single supplier is that they might start to dictate terms, because they know you rely on them only. It pays to:

- ask other people which suppliers they use;
- use the Yellow Pages or the local Chamber of Trade for

lists of alternative suppliers;
* make a note of alternative suppliers in case you need them at any stage;
* try suppliers out once or twice, so you know how they operate, and they get to know you.

*Maintenance and servicing*
Maintenance and servicing agreements are a form of insurance, as you pay for a degree of security up-front. If you intend to use machinery or equipment, always follow the manufacturers' maintenance and servicing instructions.

Do the simple things that the manual tells you, like keeping items clean, topping up fluids, or replacing component parts that wear out quickly. Try to carry out routine maintenance tasks yourself. Also, book in services by a qualified engineer at appropriate intervals.

You may want to lease equipment instead of buying it. For example, buying a photocopier means that you have to buy toner cartridges, and pay for any maintenance and repairs when the copier is no longer under guarantee. With a leased copier it is fairly normal practice to pay a tiny premium (say 1p a copy) which covers replacement toner, routine servicing and breakdown repairs. This allows you to spread costs more evenly.

A quick warning. If you enter into a long lease for equipment which you subsequently find you no longer need, you remain liable for rental commitments until the lease expires.

# 3 FINANCIAL MATTERS

## Raising finance for a business

Most people starting a business from home need either an overdraft or a business loan. You should consider the implications of each carefully.

---

**OVERDRAFT**
- you pay only when you are in the red (and possibly a one-off set-up charge);
- the interest rates are higher;
- generally smaller sums than loans.

**LOAN**
- you pay off a loan every month, whether or not you need it;
- the interest rates are lower than for overdrafts;
- there may be financial penalties if you pay off a loan early.

---

*Remember*

Most banks offer some form of free or reduced business banking to new businesses. Shop around. Banks are in business themselves and if one will not give you what you need, try another.

Anyone lending you money for a business will want to see at least four things:

- a business plan that sets out what you plan to do, what your expertise is, what market research you have done etc. (banks all provide information packs for small business, with sample forms and details of what they expect to see);

- some form of collateral to guarantee money lent by the bank, e.g. a second mortgage, a guarantor, etc.;
- some financial commitment from you;
- a cashflow forecast (page 100) to show your financial planning.

You should produce a business plan and a cashflow forecast anyway, as part of your planning. The level of collateral and your financial commitment is between you and the bank, and will be negotiated. Think carefully, though, before signing a second mortgage to guarantee a loan of a few hundred pounds. You could lose your home for this trivial amount.

Wherever possible, start with your own savings. You lose interest on these, but you pay out interest on a loan anyway.

## Will the business pay?

There is no point in running your own business if it does not produce the level of income you need. Unless you have a second income, and do it as a hobby.

There are some key aspects of finance that you need to look at. Failure to forecast costs and income fairly accurately will give you problems later on. You should look at:

- start-up costs – what it will take to get going and to survive until people start to pay you;
- running costs, split into fixed and variable costs;
- the break-even point;
- the prices you will charge.

These figures will help you to produce a cashflow forecast – something a bank will expect to see if you are borrowing money.

## Start-up costs

These are one-off costs that need to be met before the business can operate. You may need to get finance from a bank for these, in addition to any loan or overdraft arrangements you want to look after running costs. For example:

- money needed to do any home conversions;
- money to buy raw materials;
- equipment purchase. e.g. telephones, fax machine, desk, etc.;
- any professional fees, e.g. solicitors, accountants, company registration;
- business stationery, advertising leaflets, etc.;
- money to bridge the gap between doing work and getting paid.

Start-up costs don't include items for which you spread the cost for over a longer period such as leasing a photocopier. These costs are fixed costs (page 94). Don't under-estimate start-up costs.Make a list of all the items you need to get started. Visualise yourself working at home for a few typical days. Then prioritise the list; cross off any items that you can do without initially, e.g. use a table as a desk, receive faxes via an agency, etc..

## Running costs

Running costs fall into two categories:
- fixed costs, which you have to pay no matter what;
- variable costs, which change with the amount of work.

*Fixed costs*

You must budget for fixed costs whether they are daily, weekly, monthly or annual; just as you do for electricity, gas and food bills. A major benefit of working from home is that the fixed costs of a business are generally much lower. The fixed costs include:
- rent;
- rates;
- electricity;
- national insurance contributions (page 121);
- purchase of equipment, machinery, if by installments;
- interest charges on bank loans, etc.;
- any insurance premiums;
- wages you pay yourself (known as 'drawings');
- any wages you pay to regular employees.

Try to limit fixed costs as much as possible.

*Variable costs*

These vary according to the amount of work. If you make desserts for local restaurants, and you get more orders you need to spend more on ingredients, and delivery.

Generally, it is harder to cut variable costs than fixed costs. However, you can:
- buy at a better price from existing suppliers;
- use alternative materials or suppliers;
- avoid waste, by getting things right first time.

Electricity can have a variable cost element as well as a fixed cost element (the standing charge and the basic amount of electricity needed for light and heat). If you use electricity in some way to fulfil orders you will use more electricity when busy.

Both fixed and variable costs influence when a business is in profit, and both costs are needed to construct a cashflow forecast (page 100).

## Pricing

There are two main factors to consider when setting prices:
- what the market will stand;
- what you need to charge to make a profit.

*Market factors*

In virtually all cases, if you price 'high' customers will not pay it. The only exception to this is if you specialise in 'designer' goods or services. However, it is equally important not to price too low. If something is too cheap customers may perceive it as sub-standard. Your market research (page 53) should identify the price range at which you should aim for. Customers expect to pay somewhere around the middle of the range.

Avoid charging very low prices just to gain a foothold in business. It is much harder to raise prices later, and keep customers. If you have to charge lower prices to get into a market, consider publishing a higher, *full* price, and stating that your *actual* price is a special, introductory discount, for a limited period. This helps condition customers into thinking they are getting a one-off bonus.

*Pricing for a profit*

To set your prices, start by identifying the break-even point. This is the point at which you make enough money to avoid making a loss, but not enough to make a profit. It helps to set this out as a graph, so you can quickly see how many sales you need to make, and at what price, to ensure a profit.

Take for example a business that produces advertising flyers for local firms. The *product* is six master copies of the flyer (for photocopying) plus a computer disk from which the customer can print more masters.

1 The first task is to set a period in which to analyse profitability; say one month.
2 Now add up
– all daily and weekly costs (e.g. post, transport) to give a monthly total;
– all annual costs (e.g. insurance) and divide these by 12 to give a monthly total.

This gives fixed, monthly costs:

| | |
|---|---|
| electricity | £30 |
| transport | £120 |
| national insurance | £30 |
| other insurance | £100 |
| drawings (wages) | £250 |
| postage | £20 |
| computer lease | £100 |
| TOTAL | £650 |

3 Estimate the variable cost of each order:

| | |
|---|---|
| paper for masters | £1 |
| floppy disc | £1 |
| travel to client | £9 |
| electricity | £2 |
| packing and delivery | £3 |
| stationery, postage, etc. | £1 |
| TOTAL | £17 |

4 Draw a graph (Figure 2) of monthly costs (vertical axis) versus monthly orders (horizontal axis). Draw a horizontal line (A) to represent the fixed costs (£650), and plot a second for the sum of the fixed costs and the variable costs (B).

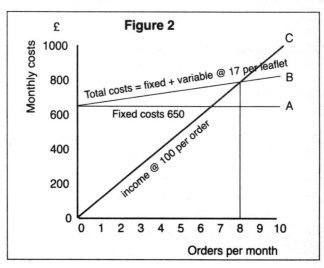

Figure 2

From the graph you can see that even with no orders, total costs are £650. For one order they are £650 + £17 = £667; for two orders £684, etc.

5 Finally, calculate the **potential income.** Market research shows that customers are willing to pay £80-£150 for the flyers. Let's test a price of £100, and plot a line for potential income (price times orders) against number of orders (C).

The **break-even point** is where the line for potential income (C) crosses the line for total costs (B), i.e. at eight orders (in fact this shows a small profit of £14).

The graph can save a lot of arithmetic as you can see that seven orders gives a loss, and nine orders and over, begins to show a tidy profit.

*Testing costs and prices*
You can use a graph like Figure 2 to see what effect different prices and costs have on profit. Figure 3 shows what happens if fixed costs are reduced by £100 a month. The break-even point is now around seven orders a month. Figure 4 shows what happens if fixed costs are kept the same, but a price of £115 is set. Now, seven orders a month produces a small profit.

So what should be done? Raise prices or cut costs, or both? Higher prices may produce fewer customers, so cutting costs is preferable. Start by looking for ways to cut fixed costs. This lowers the cost base straight away. However, don't lower the price too far, as it reduces the rate of profit growth once you have passed break-even point.

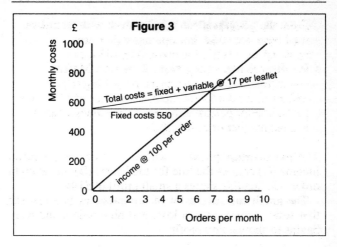

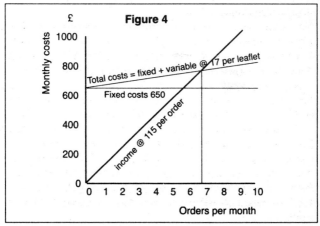

## What a cashflow forecast does

A cashflow forecast anticipates when money *actually* leaves and enters the business. This is not the same as when bills arrive or are sent. Your bank statement is a useful analogy as it shows exactly when you are credited or debited money; not when you actually write cheques, or spend cash. To forecast cashflow you have to 'best guess' when you expect to pay out money, and receive money.

Speaking of banks, the cashflow forecast is a piece of evidence that the bank manager will want from you if you need a loan or an overdraft for the business.

You need to do a cashflow forecast as you cannot afford to run out of money when you have bills to pay. **Cashflow problems are the death of many businesses**.

Take this example:
- X works from home, and arranges an overdraft of £3,000 to pay for materials;
- next month an expected cheque does not arrive, which means delaying payment on the overdraft, and a bill from a supplier Y;
- supplier Y waits patiently, but soon insists on payment;
- X still doesn't receive the cheque, and the bank refuses to extend the overdraft;
- desperate, X writes a £1,000 cheque for supplier Y;
- the cheque bounces: X gets charged £20 for this; her reputation with the bank and supplier Y plummets; supplier Y refuses to supply any more materials;
- X is unable to fulfil orders without new materials, and the business folds.

A watch-word here is 'unexpected'. A cashflow forecast should aim to reduce or remove the element of surprise with regard to money flowing into and out of the business. Also, a cashflow forecast can be monitored month-by-month, to see if it is performing to expectation, so that any potential problems can be nipped in the bud.

## How to do a cashflow forecast
This is a relatively simple process, where attention to detail and realism are the key issues:

1 Draw up a chart like Figure 5. You should include 12 months, but space does not allow us to do so.
2 List all your expected income, fixed costs and variable costs in the left-hand column. Include all costs for the coming year, to the best of your knowledge. For each month, fill in expected bills and income. If in doubt, it is better to over-estimate costs and under-estimate income.

Think carefully about any fixed costs, such as quarterly phone bills, and estimate their likely size. Also, estimate how income will vary over the year. Remember to take into account any seasonal trends, e.g. toymakers experience an increase in production costs just before Christmas, and higher income in January and February as customers settle invoices.

3 For each month calculate the total outgoings and the total income. Then work out the cashflow for each month. If more money comes into the business than goes out, the cashflow is positive (+). If the opposite is true, cashflow is negative (–).

**FIGURE 5  SAMPLE CASHFLOW FOR TOYMAKER**

| ITEM | MAY | JUNE | JULY |
|---|---|---|---|
| *Income* | | | |
| Bank loan/overdraft | 3,000 | — | — |
| Income from sales | — | 1,000 | 1,400 |
| Cash injection from savings | 1,500 | | |
| *Total income* | 4,500 | 1,000 | 1,400 |
| *Outgoings* | | | |
| **Fixed costs** | | | |
| Drawings (wages) | 300 | 300 | 300 |
| National Insurance | 30 | 30 | 30 |
| Electricity | 120 | 120 | 120 |
| Van lease | 140 | 140 | 140 |
| Telephone | — | 80 | — |
| Insurance: accident | 15 | 15 | 15 |
| Insurance: equipment | 200 | — | — |
| **Variable costs** | | | |
| Tools | 700 | 100 | — |
| Raw materials | 175 | 190 | 265 |
| Diesel | 40 | 45 | 50 |
| Van service | — | — | 120 |
| *Total outgoings* | −1,720 | −1,020 | −1,030 |
| **Total income (from above)** | +4,500 | +1,000 | +1,400 |
| **Total outgoings** | −1,720 | −1,020 | −1,030 |
| **Monthly cashflow** | +2,780 | −20 | +370 |
| **Cumulative cashflow** | | | |
| *(last cumulative plus | | (+2,780−20 ) | (+2,760+370) |
| current month)* | +2,780 | +2,760 | +3,130 |

**Remember:**
- The amounts in a cashflow forecast need to be entered for the months when they are *actually* paid in or out, not when they are invoiced or billed. Sales income in May is nil, because none of the invoices sent out in May will be settled in this month . Even then the toymaker has split the £2,400 expected over June and July, because some people will be late payers. The quarterly telephone bill arrives at the end of May, but it will be paid in June.
- Some items are monthly, some quarterly, others annual. Enter amounts for these when they are actually paid.
- Some figures go up and down, month by month. There is a higher figure for materials in May than June, because not everything bought in May will be used. A bigger top-up is necessary in July.
- The totals show the monthly picture and the ongoing picture.

The trend is what really matters. The cumulative cashflow – the bottom line – is the way you expect the bank balance to look at the end of that month. Cashflow should be climbing from the red into the black, month by month, even if it dips occasionally when a large bill has to be paid.

## Tax

The subject of tax can strike abject terror into the heart of most individuals. It need not. Coping with tax is largely a matter of keeping good records and, above all, being honest. You are then well-placed to complete essential forms and documents relating to tax.

It is worth considering getting an accountant to do your tax return, as he or she may save you more money than their fee. They know the tax system and how to deal with it in the most cost-efficient way. However, the more you know about tax yourself, and the less you leave trivial work to an accountant, the lower their fee.

---

**WARNING**

Tax laws can quickly date and are open to interpretation, so don't rely solely on this book for guidance. Check everything with the appropriate authority.

---

## Never just ignore tax

Anyone deciding to work from home must tackle tax head on. Ignoring tax and hoping it will go away leads to chaos, and probably a larger tax bill. The Tax Office is there to help you (yes, really!), so never be afraid to ask for help. Remember, you're only likely to get into trouble with tax inspectors if you deceive them.

Instead keep thorough records and be honest about your earnings. This will help you to:

• keep tabs on your business finances: how much money you have, what you owe, and what you are owed;

• avoid retrospective assessment, and pay less tax.

## Where to start

The first thing to do is to get advice. Tax regulations vary depending on whether you are employed or self-employed.

Figuring out your employment status is not always obvious – and sometimes you may be both! The Inland Revenue Leaflet *Employed or Self-employed? IR56* will help you with this.

*If you are self-employed*
There are lots of tax advantages to being self-employed, but you need to know how to make the most of them. There are numerous sources of *free* advice:
**Local tax office**
• listed in the telephone book under Inland Revenue (IR);
• gives advice on anything and everything to do with tax;
• wide range of free leaflets available – ask for the Inland Revenue's *Catalogue of Leaflets and Books* for a complete list; should also be available at your local library or Citizen's Advice Bureau; *Starting your own Business (ref. CW1)* is particularly useful, and includes details on tax, National Insurance and VAT.

**Department of Trade and Industry (DTI)**
• telephone the DTI Small Firms Section on 0171 510 0169;
• gives advice on setting up a small business; ask for their *Guide to help for small firms*. This includes an excellent flow-chart setting out everything you need to do to comply with the law.

**Your bank manager**
• the main High Street banks usually have small business advisers, and produce packs which are intended to help people get started in business (Lloyds Bank's *Small*

*Business Guide* is especially good – see Chapter 6).

## Training and Enterprise Council (TEC)/Local Enterprise Companies in Scotland (LEC)
• gives advice on setting up a new business (including tax), and where to get advice locally.

## Business Link (also known as One Stop Shops)
• government funded centres where you can get advice from local Chambers of Commerce, TECs and Enterprise Agencies all in one place; telephone Central Office on 0114 259 7507.

## Customs & Excise
• for all VAT related enquiries; telephone Customs & Excise Department: VAT Enquiries.

## Citizens Advice Bureau
• gives general advice about your legal responsibilities and tax; telephone your local office.

## The Federation of Small Businesses
• lobbying organisation for small businesses and the self-employed. Regular newsletter and access to professional advice available on membership; telephone 01253 720911.

## Prince's Youth Business Trust
(for 18-29 year olds only; 30 if disabled)
• gives advice on every aspect of setting up your own business at home; telephone 0171 543 1200.

**Self-employed friends**
Ask them how they handle their tax affairs. You could also ask a friendly accountant or solicitor.

*If you are employed*
Your employer should provide all the advice you need. Employees working from home should double-check the tax implications of this. There are tax advantages – but there can also be disadvantages, if you don't charge expenses to your employer in the right way.

*If you are both self-employed and employed*
If you do self-employed work and *also* work for an employer, you need to contact the National Insurance Inspector at your local DSS Office for advice.

# What should you do first?

*10 things to do*
Self-employed people working from home are responsible for their own tax affairs. If you are going to be self-employed:
- write and tell the Tax Office – either the one you paid tax to in your last job or your local tax office;
- fill out and send form 41G to the Tax Office – get this from the Inland Revenue booklet *Starting in Business (IR28)* or from your local tax office;
- decide on your accounting date – a fixed date when you will work out your business profits for the year – you will need to give this in form 41G; it's simplest to stick to the official tax year (6 April to 5 April the

following year). However, you can choose a different
date to complete your annual accounts – maybe when
trade is slack, or the anniversary of your business.
Under self-assessment (page 113) you will pay tax
twice yearly (31 January and 31 July) regardless of the
date you complete your annual accounts;
- send your P45 to the Tax Office (if you have given up
your previous employment);
- tell the DSS about your self-employed status, so that
they can sort out your National Insurance payments;
Fill in form CF11 *Notification of self-employment*,
available from your local DSS office, or the
Contributions Agency (part of the DSS), Class 2
Group, Longbenton, Newcastle-upon-Tyne NE98 1YX;
- speak to your local VAT Office to find out whether you
should register for VAT (page 114).

And (including employees working from home):
- open a separate business bank account, even if your
turnover may be small, as it's useful to put away some
money each month to pay the end-of-year tax bill (ask
the Inland Revenue about their Tax Deposit Scheme);
- set up a system to record and monitor all your financial
affairs – a simple accounts book, or (if you prefer) an
off-the-shelf computer package; keep copies of *all* your
invoices, bills and receipts;
- record all your expenses, e.g. equipment purchases,
travel including running costs of a car, postage,
maintenance of any equipment, training costs, etc.;
- set aside a few minutes each week to update your
financial records.

*5 things to keep*

Whether you're employed or self-employed you will need to keep thorough records of your finances – especially with the advent of self-assessment. Tax officers may ask to see these to confirm that your tax return is correct. Get used to keeping and regularly filing the following (there may be others that are important too):

- all your business invoices and receipts;
- copies of all work related bills paid;
- receipts for all business expenses – remember to ask for receipts for train tickets, petrol, any food you eat while away on business, etc.. Note everything down in a day book or on the back of the receipt, so you remember what they were for. If you forget to ask for a receipt, try to get a retrospective one. Keep them safe. Be aware that if you eat less than five miles from your home and claim it as a business expense, you will be taxed on it, as a benefit of employment!
- back-up records to show where your income came from and where expenditure went to, e.g. bank statements, cheque books (don't forget to fill in the cheque stubs), and paying in slips;
- an up-to-date filing system for all your financial records.

You will find more ideas for organising your work records in Chapter 5.

*If in doubt ...*

Tell everyone and keep everything! In time you will get used to the tax system and what it requires of you. Until then, it's worth erring on the side of caution. If things go wrong, you are very unlikely to get into trouble, if you can prove that mistakes were genuine and that you have kept careful records.

# What next?
You need to get to grips with:
• the types of tax you will have to pay;
• how to pay tax.

If you are self-employed you have to pay tax on your profits, i.e. what is left after you have deducted allowable costs. The Inland Revenue calls this taxable profit. There are two main types of tax:
• direct tax – e.g. Income, Capital Gains, Corporation and Inheritance tax;
• indirect tax – including VAT, Customs & Excise, stamp duties.

# Income tax
Simply, a tax on any income you earn or acquire. Any one who has an income over a certain amount (see Tax rates, page 111) in a tax year pays the income tax rate on that amount. For the self-employed, 'earnings' means the amount left after allowances.

*Personal allowance*
The amount of money you can earn before you pay income tax. This amount is revised annually. You can get a table outlining allowances for individuals, married couples and other special cases from your tax office.

*Tax rates*
At the time of writing there are 3 tax bands. The amount you earn in a tax year will determine which band you belong to. In September 1996 these were:
1 Lower rate of 20%    (On earnings of £0–3,900);
2 Basic rate of 24%    (On earnings of £3,901–25,500);
3 Higher rate of 40%    (On earnings of £25,500+).

*Capital Gains Tax (CGT)*
You pay capital gains tax when something you own (an asset):
• is given away, exchanged, sold or disposed of in some other way, and
• has increased value since you acquired it.

For example, if you buy a business for £50,000 and then sell it for £70,000, you may pay CGT on the profit you make, depending on whether the profit is above or below a certain threshold (around £6,300 at the time of writing). If your asset loses value, you can usually set it off against gains your business makes in the same tax year. Typical examples of things you may pay CGT on are:
• stocks and shares;
• land and property;
• the sale or transfer of your business and trading stock.
You may be liable for CGT if:
• you work from home;
• claim a proportion of general house costs, as an allowance, because part of the house is used for work;
• the value of your home is higher when you come to sell it.

Husbands and wives are each entitled to their own exempt amount. Check the current rate of exemption with your local Tax Enquiry Centre. Special rules apply when you are in a partnership, so check this out too.

The Inland Revenue leaflet *Capital Gains Tax CGT14* contains information on this subject, but it is a complex tax area, so always seek professional advice.

*Inheritance tax*
At the time of writing you can inherit up to £200 000 tax free. Above this amount you pay tax at a flat rate of 40%. Check the latest rates with your Tax Enquiry Centre.

*Corporation tax*
If you set up a limited company you have to pay corporation tax on the pre-tax profits. At the time of writing the corporation tax rate is 25% if profits are below £300 000, or 40% for higher figures.

If a dividend is paid to shareholders during the year, the company pays Advance Corporation Tax (ACT) at the appropriate rate. ACT is taken into account at the end of the tax year. The income received by a shareholder is part of their personal income, and is liable for income tax.

*VAT*
Value Added Tax (VAT) is charged on the sale or supply of most goods or services (including exchanges and gifts in kind). At the time of writing the VAT rate is 17.5% (Check with Customs & Excise for the latest rate and details of exemptions.) We look at VAT in more detail on page 114.

# Self-assessment of tax

From 6 April 1997 the self-employed will pay tax under the self-assessment system. The Government has been introducing this new system since 1994. It aims to make paying tax easier to understand, do and cope with financially.... a very laudable idea! There are two main changes to the old system. Under self-assessment:

- self-employed people pay tax on the current financial year's earnings, instead of paying tax based on the previous year's earnings;
- self-employed people pay tax in two annual installments (31 January and 31 July);

and either,

- the Tax Office sends you a tax return each April which you fill in for the preceding financial year (e.g. you pay the tax due for 1997–98 in 1998). The Tax Office uses your return and accounts to assess how much income, CGT and Class 4 NI you owe, and send you the bill;

or

- under self-assessment, you estimate your own tax payment (although the tax office will still calculate your tax for you if you ask). You make two payments on account towards your tax bill each year in January and July. Finally, you pay the balance of any tax due (or indeed, receive any overpayments back) the following January. If you opt for self-assessment you need to keep your records for five years.

# Tax deductible expenses

These are items of expenditure that the Inland Revenue regard as genuine expenses incurred in running a business or doing a job. Employees are allowed far fewer tax-deductible expenses than are the self-employed.

Allowable business expenses include:
- raw materials and supplies for the business;
- publicity and advertising (including gifts up to £10);
- most fixed costs (electricity, telephone, rent, etc.);
- bank charges and interest;
- professional fees (accountants, lawyers etc.);
- travel and vehicle costs;
- a proportion of home expenses, because part of the home is used for the business, e.g. building repairs;
- tools and equipment;
- servicing and maintenance of equipment;
- employees' wages, fees paid to subcontractors, etc.

Major items of equipment, machinery, vehicles etc., are treated separately as capital allowances. Generally a proportion of the cost of these is allowed each year, as they depreciate over a set life-span that follows an Inland Revenue formula. There are several items you cannot claim for, including:
- your drawings (wages);
- non-business expenses (i.e. personal things to do with your own private life);
- taking people to lunch, or other entertainment;
- the cost of challenging a tax assessment, interest on late tax payments, taxes themselves;

## More about VAT

VAT is paid by customers on the goods and services he or she buys. Everyone pays VAT at some point. However, businesses that are VAT registered can claim back the VAT on goods and services they buy during the course of their business.

*How VAT operates*
VAT differs from other taxes in several ways. For one, VAT is covered by criminal law as opposed to income tax which is subject to civil law. Infringement of VAT is a criminal offence because the VAT you collect from customers is not your money; it belongs to HM Customs & Excise. If you owe income tax the Inland Revenue may sue you for payment, but with VAT you have a responsibility to ensure you keep enough cash available to pay HM Customs & Excise.

When you are VAT registered you pay VAT on eligible goods and services you buy. These are 'inputs'. You tend to process these things, adding value and then sell them on at a higher price. So-called 'outputs'. The difference between the price of the inputs and the price of the outputs (excluding VAT) is the added value. This amount is subject to VAT at the current rate.

VAT is payable in various ways, either based on what is actually paid out and received – known as cash accounting – or quarterly in arrears, by
1 adding together all the VAT paid (input tax);
2 adding together all the VAT charged to customers (output tax);
3 subtracting input tax from output tax (the VAT due).

The amount due is normally a positive figure, as most businesses collect more VAT than they pay. If the amount due is negative, Customs & Excise sends you a cheque or credits your account. This is most likely in the start-up period of a business.

*An example*
- X is offered 1,000 teddy bears at £1 each.
- X pays 17.5% VAT on the bears, i.e. £175.
- X also buys 1,000 boxes to display the bears in, at 10p each (£100), and again pays VAT on the amount (£17.50).
- X has therefore paid £1,100 to buy the goods, plus £192.50 in VAT.
- X adds value by selling the boxed bears, individually, at £2 each, plus VAT (35p) – total £2.35.
- X sells all the bears and collects £350 in VAT.
  X therefore owes the Customs & Excise £157.50 (£350 minus £192.50).

X effectively acts as a collector of taxes for the Customs & Excise, which oversees VAT. (This example has been simplified, as it does not include VAT that the sole trader is paying out on general overheads.)

*When you should register*
HM Customs & Excise issues regular updates on the rules for registration, in line with changes decided by the Government. Their *VAT notes 4, 1995*, specifies when registration is compulsory:

From midnight on 28 November 1995 you will have to be registered if:
- at the end of any month the value of the taxable supplies you have made in the past 12 months has

exceeded £47,000, or
• at any time there are reasonable grounds for believing that the value of the taxable supplies you will make in the next 30 days will exceed £47,000.

*Voluntary registration*
Even if your income is less than the limit stated above, you may still choose to register for VAT. This way, you can claim back:
• some of your start up costs (only if they arose less than 6 months before registering);
• VAT on your supplies.
However, the down side is:
• doing your VAT accounts;
• your prices go up in effect, as you have to charge VAT – but if your customers are registered too, nobody feels the pain!

Voluntary VAT registration is a personal matter based on your own circumstances, However, it may be worth considering voluntary registration if one or more of the following factors applies to you:
• all your customers are VAT registered;
• your business will send out relatively few invoices;
• you pay VAT on a lot of inputs.

You won't be able to register for VAT if you supply only exempt items. What this means is explained below.

*How to register*
Contact your local VAT Office (ring HM Customs &

Excise to get the number) to find out if you should register for VAT. If the answer is yes, you will need to complete some forms, after which you will be given:
• a VAT registration number;
• a registration date – from this date you *must* charge VAT.

*Zero rating and exemption*
Some goods and services are exempt from VAT or zero rated. Zero-rated items are liable for VAT, but the government sets their rate at 0%. Newspapers, books, cold food (but not catering) and children's clothes are zero-rated (at the time of writing). There is a reduced VAT rate on domestic fuel and power.

Examples of VAT-exempt items are:
• certain education and training;
• insurance and financial services;
• doctors', dentists' and opticians' services.

## Some common questions answered

*What is an income tax year?*
The official tax year runs from 6 April to 5 April the following year.

If you don't file your business accounts at the end of March/beginning of April each year, you will be taxed on the profits for your accounting year which ends in the current tax year – so if your accounting date is 30 June 1998, you will settle the balance of your tax payment for the official tax year 1997/98 on 31 July 1998.

*What happens after a budget?*
There are usually changes to the tax situation. Most
changes will be self-apparent in your tax return. If you
are unsure about anything ask your local Tax Office for
advice.

*What if you don't complete a tax return or pay any tax?*
You can be fined. If you pay too little or no tax on the due
date, you will be charged interest on the difference, from
the date it is due. You will also be charged a 5%
surcharge on any tax unpaid by 28 February (once month
after tax date).

*What if your business loses money?*
You may not have to pay any tax.

Say you make a loss of £10,000 in year 1, and a profit
of £8,000 in year 2. Instead of paying tax on your £8,000
profit, you can carry forward the loss you made in year 1.
Result – you don't pay any tax that year. You can carry
forward losses until they are used up.

You can also offset losses against other forms of
income such as share dividends, an inheritance, etc.

## Employees and tax

'Working from home can actually increase tax liabilities
if workers are not careful,' according to David Sinton of
Deloitte & Touche 'but those who plan correctly should
see some savings'.

There are some points to think about, *before* you start working from home as an employee:

- get a written instruction to work from home from your employer – if the move is personal choice you can't claim for equipment, travel or domestic expenses;
- check with your employer whether you need to tell the DSS you are working from home;
- personal use of office equipment – if your employer's office equipment is ever used for personal reasons (e.g. letters, household accounts) this is a taxable perk.
- phone calls:
- if you are going to use the phone a lot ask your employer to install a separate business line; that way they can reimburse all your calls and line rental without either of you being taxed;
- make a note of all business calls you make on your home line;
- beware – cash reimbursement for phone calls can make you and your employer liable for extra National Insurance payments;
- travel costs – you can claim a trip to your employer's office as business travel; your employer can reimburse these travel expenses, tax free;
- council tax and mortgage interest – you can't usually claim any tax relief on these. If you buy a larger home because you needed a dedicated office at home, you might have some grounds. Check with your Tax Office. The flip side of dedicated office space is that you can lose out on capital gains tax relief when selling the house. Simply working 'somewhere' in the home means you can get tax relief on the whole property.

## National Insurance

### Full-time employees

Your National Insurance (NI) contributions will continue to be deducted automatically from your wage packet via PAYE. The employer also makes a contribution on your behalf.

### Self-employed

*Who do you contact?*

Ask your National Insurance Inspector at the DSS Contributions Agency for an information pack (ring Social Security: Department of, or the Social Security Advice Line, Freephone 0800 393 539). You will need to:

- fill out the 'declaration of self-employment form' (CF11);
- choose how to pay your NI (weekly, monthly).

Even if you continue to work as an employee, check things out with your local Social Security Office. If you have any questions or queries contact the National Insurance Inspector. Have your National Insurance number to hand. If you can't find it, ask your local Social Security Office for it.

*How do the self-employed pay NI?*

Self-employed people usually pay two types of NI contributions:

- flat rate, Class 2 contributions – around £6 per week (including holiday weeks); these can be paid weekly or monthly by direct debit to the DSS, or you can ask to

pay a quarterly bill (issued in January, April, July and October). Generally NI increases by 15p or so after each budget;
• Class 4 contributions – based on your earnings at the end of the tax year, these are collected by the Inland Revenue when you pay income tax.

*How is Class 4 NI calculated?*
In 1996:
• You don't pay Class 4 NI on profits up £6,640. On profits of (say) £8,000 you pay 7.3% of £1,360 (£8,000 minus £6,640);
• The upper limit for Class 4 NI is £22,880 for which you pay a contribution rate of 7.3%. If your profits are above the upper limit, the maximum Class 4 NI you pay is 7.3% of £16,240 (£22,880 minus £6,640).

Part-time, employed people may also have to pay Class 1 PAYE contributions to their employers.

*When don't you pay NI contributions?*
You don't pay Class 2 contributions for any complete week (Sunday to Saturday) that you can't work because of sickness or pregnancy. This applies whether or not you are getting Incapacity Benefit or a Maternity Allowance.

Get a sick note from your doctor to prove you've been off sick – and send it to your local DSS office (Incapacity Benefits Branch if you are in N. Ireland) who will give you NI credits for the week/s you've been off sick. If you are an employee give the sick note to your employer.

## Some common questions answered

*What do you do if ... you forget to pay your National Insurance?*
Contact the DSS Contributions Agency. They will send you the forms you need to fill in and a retrospective bill. You risk prosecution if you fail to act.

*... you can't afford to pay outstanding NI payments?*
Talk to your NI Inspector who can probably arrange for you to pay the outstanding amount in installments over the next year. You may have to pay interest on the outstanding amount.

## Tax and NI when employing staff

If you employ someone to help with your work, you become responsible for aspects of their tax. You will need to deduct income tax (PAYE) and NI contributions from their wages, and also pay employer's contributions towards their NI. However, everyone can earn a certain amount, tax free each year (page 111).

*What should you do?*
As soon as you decide to employ someone:
• tell your PAYE Tax Office (your local Tax Office will give you the address);
• fill out form P223 (available from the PAYE Tax Office or in the IR leaflet *Thinking of taking someone on? IR53*);
• get a PAYE tax reference number from the PAYE Tax

office – quote this number on all related correspondence.

You will automatically receive the Inland Revenue's *New Employer's Starter Pack*. This is a step-by-step guide to everything you need to do as a new employer, and contains a series of P8 cards. These give instructions on how to pay PAYE and National Insurance contributions for your employee(s).

*Things to get from your employee(s)*
When an employee starts work ask them for their :
• P45 (send part 3 to the PAYE Office and keep part 2); if they don't have a P45 use form P46 instead (in your *New Employer's Starter Pack*);
• National Insurance number (it should be on their P45).

*Making payments*
The P8 cards give step-by-step instructions on working out your own and your employee's PAYE and NI contributions. The starter pack also contains standard pay slips. If you need further advice contact your local Tax Enquiry Office.

*Sickness and maternity*
If you ever have to pay Statutory Sickness Pay (SSP) or Statutory Maternity Pay (SMP), tax and NI will be deducted in the same way. There is information on this in the *New Employer's Starter Pack*.

*At the end of the year...*
You need to tell the PAYE Tax Office how much you have paid your employee(s) and what deductions have been made. The Tax Office will automatically send you a series of forms to fill out :
- P14 – complete one for each employee;
- P60 – a summary of tax payments: give a copy to each employee who is still with you at the end of the tax year (April 5);
- P35 – record of all details on one form: send this to your Tax Office.

*If an employee leaves...*
Simply fill out their P45 with the totals of their pay and tax for the year and then:
- send part 1 to your PAYE Tax Office;
- give parts 2 and 3 to your ex-employee.

And a final word – if you act as an employer, all employees are entitled to a statement of the terms and conditions of their employment, under the employment legislation.

# 4 PLANNING AND ORGANISING THE WORKSPACE

Workspace is a fundamental issue for anyone working at home. The key issues are:

- planning where to work and how to arrange your workplace;
- keeping your workspace and yourself secure;
- making sure that your work environment is comfortable, healthy and conducive to productive work;
- selecting the right equipment;
- hiring contractors to make any necessary alterations.

## Why plan?

All too often people start working from home without doing any planning. However, there are a number of important implications of merging two parts of your life – home and work.

You will be putting more pressure on your home, because it will be fulfilling more than one role, one of which it was probably never intended for. The home as a workplace can lead to the problems of congestion and confusion, if you are not careful. So careful planning is important.

## Congestion

Congestion is a potential difficulty for two reasons:

- you have to fit two major sets of activities (work and domestic life) into one place. Your living room may

126

double-up as an office or store room. Many people soon realise that they can't live with congestion, and quit work at home;

• congestion puts pressure on your relationships with people you live with. They may be tolerant to begin with, but after a few months patience can begin to be strained.

## Confusion

In traditional working patterns there is usually a clear divide between home and work. The important thing is not to get home life and work confused. Sensible planning can help you to distinguish between the two sets of activities, and draw a dividing line. This maintains health and happiness in the home.

At a basic level this might involve allocating certain parts of the week to work and home life, or fitting a lock to the room you work in, to reduce the likelihood of you wandering in, outside 'working hours'.

## Staying healthy

A carefully planned workspace helps to maintain health and happiness. Poorly planned space can create occupational hazards, e.g. a chair that does not support your back. A cluttered, messy or ill-thought out workspace can, over time, make you irritable, or frustrate the people you share with.

## Being considerate

You need to give careful thought as to how you manage the relationship between your work and the people you share with. There may be a brief honeymoon period in

127

which each new day is a joy, but the demands of home life and work can quickly come into conflict. For instance, it can be hard to work if:

- you have a spouse who spends most of their time at home;
- customers need to visit, or friends visit;
- there are children around.

At an early stage, it is important to negotiate with people in your life, what is and isn't acceptable about the way you do your work. This planning stage will help you and your family/friends to come to terms more rapidly with the challenges that working from home brings. The negotiation also shows that you care about what people think, and will not simply impose a whole new pattern of life on them.

## Costs

Careful planning can also save money in the long run. If you think about your security needs, equipment you will need, and how equipment will fit into your home, you can avoid unnecessary costs. For example, buying furniture you don't have space for, or having your computer stolen, along with all the information stored in it.

## Legal issues

Try to identify any legal problems you may face working at home. You may not be *allowed* to work from home (see Chapter 2).

The title deeds to your home, the lease agreement if you have one, and your mortgage agreement may all forbid you to work from home or at least limit the kind of work you can do.

As you saw earlier the chances are that if you're working from home in a way that is low impact – in other words doesn't cause real nuisance to your neighbours, then the chances are that you will be allowed to work from home. But do take advice from your planning department.

There are a whole range of things that may come up here including things like:

• you haven't got the space you need;
• there is insufficient light;
• the business will cause such a nuisance to your neighbours that there's no way you will be able to do it.

## Green light, red light?

You may find at the end of the planning process that your work is not suited to your home, even if you plan to work only two or three days from home.

But you must go through the planning process and give yourself the green light to work from home. Otherwise, your work and domestic life could get very messy.

The next section deals with how to go about this planning process.

## Assessing your needs

If you have no choice but to work at home then some of what follows may not be so relevant to you. If this is the case, we include some hints and suggestions later in this chapter.

## The methodology to use

When you assess your workspace needs:

- be realistic – don't kid yourself that things will be all right when you know they won't;
- talk to other people at home, so that:
- they feel part of the decision-making process, and can express their needs, fears and expectations;
- they can put themselves in your shoes and understand your *own* needs, fears and expectations;
- you satisfy everyone's ideas.
- give the exercise adequate time;
- ask someone you trust to go through the process.

This last point is important, and can save you a lot of time. It's often useful to run through this exercise with someone who is already working from home, preferably in a similar line of business. They will know whether your expectations are realistic.

## The steps to take

The following steps should help you through the planning process successfully. You will probably need to add other steps, but remember it is the *process* that is important.

*List all the tasks you are likely to do from home.*
Think about what your working days will be like, and list all associated tasks. For example:

- telephone calls;
- meetings at home;
- storing away items;
- packaging things up;

- typing;
- referring to books or resource material.

Don't leave anything out. Your list may be quite long. When you have completed your list you can start to get a feel for the best place in your home for work. Your list should identify times when you will deal with people, and often these are the most problematical for someone working from home. If you are likely to meet with customers at home, you will need somewhere relatively private (if this is at all possible). Customers may be put off visiting if they have to face piles of washing, or general domestic clutter. If you are going to be running a counselling service from home, you have to find somewhere comfortable, and private, to work.

Also, do you really want visitors to share the same toilet as you? If not, you may need to put in a new toilet.

*Decide who's going to be working in the house*
Is it just going to be you or will other people be working with you? If you are going to have people coming to your home, you will need to find space for them.

*Consider the family*
Are your family going to be in while you are working? Will you be able to work with their noise… and will they be able to live with your noise?

Do you need to position your workspace accordingly? You may want to separate your workspace from your family, if this is possible. If not, you may need to think about negotiating work hours, and setting some kind of

131

drill to help separate work from home life.

Some people realise early on that family and work will not fit in the same place. In many cases, their answer is to take their work out into the garden by building a shed.

But this process of thinking through how you are going to make the space work for you is a key first step to deciding where the work actually takes place.

*Decide whether you need a separate workspace*
Some types of work demand a separate workspace. For example, if you will be running an ironing service you definitely need to separate work from home, especially if you have pets. Animal hairs don't go down well on shirt collars.

While researching this book someone pointed out the example of an osteopath whose customers did not like undressing, ready for an osteopathic session, if the rest of the family were around. So if you need a separate workspace, plan it in.

*Work out how much space you need*
Come up with a maximum and minimum. If you cannot find even the minimum space then you should think again about working from home. If you can find just enough space, then further, careful planning will be needed.

*Work out how much light you are likely to need*
If you will be doing a job that involves a lot of writing or editorial work, the right level of light is very important. You may need to work in a room where more natural light comes in. Too little light is a strain on your

eyes – this can damage your eyes, and make you work less efficiently.

*Think carefully about how much noise you can tolerate*
You may decide to work at the front of the house, if there is a railway bridge running near the back. It sounds simple, but you do need to think about what the work *requires*, and what your home can *provide*.

*Think about catering arrangements*
You may need to cater for people, e.g. coffee for visitors. If the family is eating around the same time, who gets priority? You may need to draw up some rules that divide home and work life. You might even have to provide some rudimentary catering facilities for yourself during your working day.

*Consider basic issues of security*
We will look at security later, but you need to plan for it. You may be running a small mail order business, or the like, in which case there should be somewhere to keep money secure, possibly a safe.

*Reflect on your lifestyle*
You may live in a busy house that's constantly full of people – friends dropping in, relations calling around for a chat. If you do, think of the implications on your work.

*Consider the neighbours*
This is an important point and it must not be ignored. You can run into trouble with neighbours, if you don't

plan your workspace properly. For instance, if you are going to be giving singing lessons, and you set up a teaching area right next to your neighbours' wall, you will soon get complaints.

Likewise you can hit problems even with things such as typing or word processing. If you are in a flat with thin walls, and you are typing until 2 or 3 o'clock in the morning, the noise can easily carry.

## Deciding on your workspace

When you have carefully assessed your workspace needs, come up with some simple recommendations for your workspace. Use them to decide:

• which is the correct room(s) for you to work in?
• whether you need to modify your home in any way?
• what things you need to negotiate with your household?

## Be realistic

Having made decisions about the workspace you need, you are in a position to draw up some simple plans for working at home. If the results of the planning exercise show real limitations, you have three options:

• live with them;
• get over them;
• decide not to work at home.

It's important to realise that working from home is never ideal. People often think that it is, but in fact there are the same levels of compromise, annoyance and difficulties as there are working in a normal work place. One benefit of going through the planning exercise is that you rationalise your expectations. You don't opt for costly or grandiose schemes that simply won't work for you.

The bottom-line decisions, if you have decided that you will work at home are:

• what can you live with?
• what do you need to change, and how?

Armed with this insight you can go onto the next stage which is about drawing up your plan.

# Drawing up your detailed plan

This is the stage where you plan and organise your workspace in detail.

## Stick to four principles

Your aim is to achieve a workspace that allows you to function effectively. Four basic principles for this were established by Ernest J. McCormick in 1970. They have become accepted generally as the rationale for a perfect office layout.

*The Importance Principle*
The most important items should be in the most advantageous or accessible locations.

*The Frequency-of-use Principle*
The most frequently used items should be in the most advantageous or accessible locations.

*The Function Principle*
Items concerned with closely related functions or actions
should be grouped together (in large workplaces these are
often called workstations).

*The Sequence-of-use Principle*
Items which are commonly used in sequence should be
grouped together and laid out in a way which is
compatible with that sequence.

The idea that you should ideally use as little effort and
energy as possible in achieving as much as possible is
common sense. But that does not mean that workspaces
are always planned around those principles.

We might add a fifth principle: make your workspace
somewhere pleasant to work. Efficiency is important, but
if you are going to spend a lot of time somewhere, it must
be a place you like to spend time in.

## List the details
Draw up a list of furniture and equipment that you need
for your work, and split them into categories, according
to frequency of use. Ignore how small items are; even
paper clips have to be stored somewhere. There are some
examples at the top of page 137. You can change the
timescales to suit your work.

Whether you have a designated workspace or not, you
don't need to have close to hand things you use weekly or
less frequently. If you can find other places to store these
items, you will free up valuable working space.

Some things – such as previous years' ledgers, old

---

**OFTEN DURING THE DAY**
desk, personal computer, calculator, telephone
**DAILY**
stamps, answering machine, filing cabinet
**BETWEEN DAILY AND WEEKLY**
bank ledger, invoice files, vacuum cleaner
**WEEKLY OR LESS FREQUENTLY**
file bank statements, accounts

---

invoices and paperwork – will probably never be looked at again, but legally still need to be kept for a certain period. It is often best to:

- put all your redundant stuff together;
- clearly label it in case you have to refer back to it;
- put it somewhere out of the way;
- make sure that you store it somewhere dry or the paper could soon be unreadable and may rot (remember that mice and other pests like making nests out of paper!);
- make a note of the contents of each box, so that you can locate things quickly.

## Get a picture of your office

On some graph paper (A3 ideally):

- draw a scaled diagram of your workspace, and mark in doors, windows, power sockets, radiators, etc;
- make at least 10 copies;
- measure the furniture to be used (or write down approximate sizes);
- make scale cut-outs of all furniture, and move them around on the graph paper to find the best use of space

(remembering McCormick's principles, page 135);
- place work tops under natural light;
- make sure any VDU screens are at least 45 ° to windows, and are not over radiators;
- mark positions for machines (faxes, etc.); work on the principle that they are best out of the way;
- list all the items you are to work with and position each item on your plan.

## Changing basic amenities

When you are happy with your workspace layout, check to make sure that there are power sockets where they are needed. If they need to be changed or more are needed, mark the desired points in red. Every item should have its own socket.

Repeat this process for lighting (mark desired positions in green), and radiators (blue).

If you need an expert to carry out these changes, read the section appointing contractors (page 168). There may be reasons why you cannot make the changes, so now is the time to find out.

## Security

There are some very important issues concerning security that must be addressed. We touched on security in Chapter 2, but it gets special attention here. People often ignore security when they work from home, probably for the following reasons:
- they feel safe in their home;
- they feel that being at home a lot will deter thieves;

- they think that their home's, often quite rudimentary, security precautions are sufficient;

However, existing security arrangements for your home may well be inadequate when the home becomes a workplace.

## A basic review
Carry out a security review. Think of possible areas in which there may be security problems. The checklist covers some of the issues you need to consider. Give yourself a score out of 5 for each, where:
- 5 is definitely or always;
- 4 is more often than not, or probably;
- 3 is fairly often or quite possibly;
- 2 is rarely or unlikely;
- 1 is never or definitely not.

| Security Checklist | Score |
|---|---|
| Will you be holding large amounts of cash at home? | ❏ |
| Will you be holding stocks or goods relating to your business at home? | ❏ |
| Do you expect people (customers) to come into your home? | ❏ |
| Will there be other people working with you at home? | ❏ |
| Do you have gear or tools of the trade on display (e.g. in full view of the street)? | ❏ |
| Do you advertise your work, i.e. is it obvious that your work involves you holding things of value at home? | ❏ |
| How often are you going to be on your own? | ❏ |
| **Total (max. 35, min. 7)** | ❏ |

If your total score is low (say below 10) don't be *too* complacent about security, even though many of the ideas that follow here are apparently obvious. Complacency is the greatest security hazard there is.

Even with a low score there may be some particular security risks. Make these your priorities for action. You can ask your local crime prevention unit to visit your home and advise you on these matters. You can contact them via your local police station – and we recommend you do.

If you score over 18, you should go through all the security points, check what needs doing – and do it.
Some ideas for security measures are:
• if you hold valuable stocks or goods at home arrange secure storage space for them, rather than leaving them out, or trusting ordinary locks;
• if you have other people working from home – even if they are people you know –avoid putting temptation in people's way;
• if you really want a street-fronted workspace, go outside and look at it from the perspective of a passer-by; it is possible to arrange valuable items inside without giving others a full view of the interior, e.g. using curtains, blinds, lights, posters, etc.;
• advertising your work, letting people know you hold things of value in the home, working alone, and having people visit you all put you at increased risk of theft and personal harm. There are some suggestions for ways of reducing this risk in the next few pages.

# Theft and burglary

Remember, if you get broken into, and your equipment is stolen it can be a double blow:

- first, your personal space has been invaded;
- second, you have lost your means of earning a living.

Even if you are insured, you have to go through the rigmarole of replacing equipment. In the meantime, your business comes to a grinding halt. And it's a sad fact that when you have had equipment stolen once, you have a better than 50% chance of being burgled again soon. Thieves realise that many items get replaced through the insurance.

This is why it is important to think through security issues when you work from home, even if it's only part - time.

There is a range of things you can do to make your home more secure ...

*Steps you can take*
The following is a list of some ideas for making your home more secure:

- fit insurance approved locks to your front and back doors. Apart from anything else, your policy may be invalid without them. Don't forget French doors, as burglars often target these;
- never pop out for a minute, leaving doors or windows open. Opportunism is one of the main types of theft from homes. (The same is true of theft from vehicles);
- code and security mark your equipment. If you are burgled, you may be able to get your equipment back,

if the burglar is caught;
- fit strong door bolts;
- put key operated locks on all windows;
- if appropriate, plant prickly hedges around the perimeter of your property. The police say that this is one of the main deterrents against burglars. You can get more advice from your local crime prevention officer;
- consider getting a dog; it is not only a deterrent but also an early alarm system;
- fit shutters. Many properties, especially in cities, are now fitted with shutters;
- install some security lighting and consider a system where an infra-red sensor sounds an alarm to cover daylight hours;
- install a safe. For money or documents (often your information is worth far more). For documents or back-up computer disks you may want to fit a fireproof safe;
- make a note of serial numbers on equipment and take photographs of unusual items. This helps the police and insurance companies to recover or settle claims for stolen goods;
- join your local Neighbourhood Watch scheme.

The important thing is to carry out a full review to make sure that your property is as secure as possible.

## Personal security

The second aspect of security is your own personal security. Again, people tend to feel safe at home, but if you are meeting people at home, about whom you don't know much, then you are putting yourself at risk.

It is important not to worry unnecessarily about this, and get paranoid, but some simple steps can improve your personal security.

*Steps you can take*
The following is a list of some security ideas for improving your personal security:

- entry phones allow you to identify people at the door before they enter, and if you are away from the front door, it saves time;
- video entry phones and cameras are relatively expensive but will come down in price as they become more popular. If you are interested in these a specialist security firm can offer you advice on the best system.
- panic buttons offer reassurance and are practical too; When pressed they can trigger an alarm outside to alert passers-by, and inside to alarm whoever is threatening you;
- locking doors sounds obvious but often people enter homes simply because doors are open. This is a great temptation when you are working from home, particularly on a summer's day. People often leave the windows and doors open to let air in, and then go and work upstairs. This leaves you open to invasion by someone else;
- keep a note of your itinerary in your diary, particularly if you are visiting people you don't know very well. This means family and friends can check where you are, and when you should be back. If you don't return on time, they can chase you up, or contact the police;
- in addition to keeping a diary, try to let other people

know where you are and what you are doing;
- mobile phones were ridiculed when they first came out, but are now regarded as a personal security measure. Think hard about getting a mobile phone. If you do, carry it with you, especially if you are meeting with unfamiliar people. Mobile phones can be a saviour if your car breaks down;
- it is worthwhile getting a feeling for people you work with, particularly if you work in a vulnerable field such as psychotherapy, or counselling. One way of doing this is to identify so-called red, amber and green customers:
- Red people are those you are suspicious of, you feel can become angry or have become distressed with you in the past.
- Amber people are those you aren't quite sure of.
- Green people are those you are confident with, you know well or you don't think will cause you any problems.
- If you are going to meet or have in your house a red or amber person, this may be the time to keep your panic button close to you, or tell someone to keep tabs on you. One person said that whenever she has a red customer visit her at home, she makes sure that her partner is in the house.
- neighbours can be very helpful with personal security, as they can generally keep an eye on you and your home.

Remember: if you employ people to work in your home, you have a legal responsibility for their personal safety.

## Fire

People often skimp on fire precautions at home. You can
get advice on fire prevention from the Fire Protection
Association, the Health & Safety Executive, or the Royal
Society for the Prevention of Accidents. Make sure that
you take advice and act on it, before you start working
from home. Some insurance policies may be invalid, if
you don't take the right precautions.

These days, fire extinguishers and other methods of
dealing with fire are much cheaper. At the very least you
should fit smoke alarms and appropriate fire
extinguishers.

If you employ anyone, you will have to make
modifications to doors, lighting and escape routes to obey
the Fire Precautions Act. So make sure you seek advice
from the organisations mentioned above, or the Fire
Prevention Officer at your nearest fire station.

## The work environment

The correct lighting, fresh air and a low level of noise
can make the difference between working half a day,
making no progress, and feeling irritable; and working a
full, productive day, feeling satisfied, and looking
forward to starting work the next day. Remember though,
that it is your actions that can make the real difference.
However good your work environment is, if you work in
the wrong way, or take too few breaks, working from
home will turn from delight into drudgery.

In Chapter 5 we examine stress but one of the real
dangers facing people is that they spend too long

145

slogging through their work. If you spend too many hours sitting at home without moving, then you may find health risks creeping up on you. In a traditional work setting, people find time for breaks, and tend to talk, socialise, or walk around. Just because you are working at home doesn't mean that you need to give all this up.

A well-designed workspace will help you work in a healthier way, so follow the guidelines in this section.

# Lighting

One of the great benefits of working from home is that you can customise your surroundings to suit yourself. In the case of lighting, you can choose the *type* of lighting and the *level* of lighting that you need. People have different requirements of lighting, and to complicate this, the requirements change as you get older:

- by the age of 40 you need three times the level of light to carry out a given task, as you did when you were 10 years old;
- by the age of 60 this will have risen to 15 times that for a 10 year old.

The correct type and level of lighting is important because it allows you to:

- concentrate better – your eyes and brain will be more relaxed;
- work longer – bad lighting strains your eyes which will force you to stop work;
- work more comfortably – good lighting helps to create an environment that you will find pleasing to work in;
- increase your profits – if you are able to concentrate

better and work longer you will work more efficiently and effectively.

# Lighting and health

The most obvious drawback of working in bad lighting is that your health will suffer. In most jobs, you have to focus closely on your work at times which means that your eyes do a lot of work. In poor lighting your eyes can become strained and tired, possibly giving you a headache, or in extreme cases a migraine. Make your life easier by working under the right level of light.

*Sorting out the electrics*
A specific health hazard linked to lighting is the electricity it uses. Individual lights and other electrical apparatus may seem harmless, but the problem with many workplaces is that these electrical items are condensed into a fairly small area. Spread out they are low risk, but collectively they can be dangerous.

Virtually every workplace at home has too few power sockets, and the understandable answer adopted by most people is to use an extension lead. This can increase the demand on a circuit to a level it is not designed for. The risk is not just one of fire, but potentially loss of business, e.g. an overloaded socket can cause a computer to crash.

There are no real restrictions on the level, quantity or type of lighting that you use, but you should alleviate potential risks before, and during the course, of installing your lighting. These include:
• concealed wiring in a bad condition, particularly in some old houses;

- visible wiring; wires trailing along the floor, from free-standing lamps and other apparatus, will become bare if walked on continually (and they are ideal for tripping over);
- overloaded electrical circuits; every circuit has a limit to the amount of current it will carry, and it is easy to draw too much current from a single power point (home workshops which use machine tools are a particular area for concern, and may need heavy duty cables installed);
- lampshades of the wrong size or material, or light bulbs that emit a lot of heat, can cause shades to catch fire.

Obviously, if you have a tight budget you may be tempted to install the lighting yourself, and resort to a book for help. However, if you do not know what you are doing, you could quite literally put yourself out of business, or more importantly put your home and the lives of your family at risk. The installation itself may be quite straightforward, but it is essential that the wiring is tested both before and after the installation by a qualified and certified electrician, or your local electricity board. The worst way to find out that you have made a mistake is as a result of a fire caused by your faulty wiring!

The best advice is to employ a qualified electrician to wire lights for you, preferably one who has public liability insurance cover.

## Bright is not always right

Too many people assume that bright lighting is essential to efficient work, and install rows of fluorescent lights above their workspace. People often find that they cannot work as comfortably, and as efficiently as they hoped in bright lighting.

Look around your home to see how effective lighting is a matter of careful judgement. The type of lights and their wattage is generally chosen to suit the activity normally carried out in the room, such as:
• reading lamps by the bed;
• low-wattage lights in the eating area;
• spotlights in the kitchen.

You probably take great pleasure in selecting lights for domestic purposes, so you should adopt the same approach when deciding on your workplace lighting. Whether you intend to work in one place all day, or move around, doing different tasks, you need to work out the most appropriate type and level of light. There are three essential elements in a suitable lighting system:
• the right quality and type of light;
• good distribution of light;
• the correct type of lamp or light fitting.

## Light quality

A common misconception is that the only perfect source of light is natural, and that any other form is a poor substitute. Wherever possible you should aim to make the best use of natural light, but as the evening draws in, the light fades. In any case, you may need to use artificial light during the day.

This does not mean that you have to accept inferior light quality. There are many sources of expertise on lighting, including specialist engineers and photographers, who can help to recreate the quality of natural light. Jeremy Myerson in his book *Better Lighting* defines the basic elements of an efficient and aesthetically pleasing lighting design as:

- the light source: the quantity of light that the bulb emits;
- the light fixture: its aesthetic appearance and the way this instrument controls, directs and distributes light;
- the position of the light fixture.

You need to consider each of these and, at the end of this section, you will find advice on assessing your lighting requirements, and choosing lights to suit your work.

## Types of lighting

There are four types of lighting in common use:

- general or background lighting, which is a substitute for natural light and enables people to move around safely. This lighting is usually supplemented by other forms of lighting. Wall lights, table lamps and uplights when used for background lighting generally produce a more interesting effect than a standard overhead bulb;
- task lighting, which provides light needed to perform specific jobs. Eyestrain can be avoided by selecting the type of lighting that suits the task in hand. Downlights, flexible desk lamps and spotlights are typically used for task lighting;
- accent lighting is used to highlight displays and aesthetically pleasing objects, and to create a particular atmosphere. Apart from the more commonly used

spotlights, very pleasing effects can be created by using floor-standing uplights;
• information or utility lighting is commonly used in buildings for safety purposes. This includes lights that illuminate stairways and darkened areas in case of fire. Flashing beacons at zebra crossings are an example of information lighting.


*Light distribution*
No matter what type of lighting you use, it is important to select the right light *fitting*, to control the distribution of the light from its source. The three main categories of light distribution are:
• omni-directional, where light is dispersed in all directions, such as from an overhead fitting with a lantern shade which gives background light;
• semi-directional, where light is directed mainly in one direction but is also diffused in other directions to a small degree; such as a table lamp which is being used for task lighting;
• directional light is focused specifically in one direction, e.g. a spotlight. Multiple spotlights can disperse directional light to more than one point from one fitting.


To distribute light around your workspace effectively, you should refer back to your workspace plan (page 137), and make decisions about the kind of lighting you will need to carry out work orientated tasks.

*Light fixtures*

Light fixtures enable you to distribute light in the way that you want. Having decided on the type of lighting and lighting distribution, you can then decide which fixtures to use in order to achieve the best results. You will need to find the right balance between:

- the shape of the fitting that will give the right distribution;
- the shade and colour that you would like to have around you.

Take your plan to a lighting specialist who should have a very good idea of what you need. Alternatively, any good lighting shop will send someone to visit you and make some suggestions. (They may also be able to wire and fit the lights).

*Types of light fixture*

Hanging lights are the most common lighting fixture. They give omni-directional, semi-directional or directional light, depending on the shade used. Other types of fixture include:

- wall lights
- downlights
- floor lamps
- strip lighting
- wall washers
- uplights
- table lamps
- curiosity lights
- ceiling lights
- spotlights
- desk lights

Together with the light fitting and shade, the correct bulb will give you the quantity, colour and quality of light that you want. Bulbs come in a vast range of shapes and sizes to cater for the variety of fittings that are on the market.

They also come in different wattages to suit each situation.

*Light levels*
There are two terms used by professionals when they measure light levels. It may be useful for you to be familiar with these, when you consult lighting specialists:
• lumen: a measure of the concentration of light arriving at a given surface from a given direction.
• lux: the number of lumens per square metre.
It may be easier and more helpful to remember that:
• 500 lux is considered to be suitable for general lighting in office areas;
• 750 lux is more suitable for detailed work such as reading.

## Assessing and choosing lighting

The aim of this exercise is to mark a copy of your workspace plan with the type of lighting and distribution that you need, including where lights should be.

On a copy of your plan, mark the kind of light fittings and the most appropriate bulbs that you need to give you the correct light. Use the following steps:
• identify the activities you will be carrying out and mark them in appropriate places on your plan;
• referring to the section on 'Light quality' (page 149) write down next to your activities the quality of light that you will need to perform them;
• referring to the section on 'Types of lighting' write down the most appropriate light for each activity;
• referring to the section on 'Light Distribution' put in

how you think the light would be best distributed for the activity;
- referring to the section on 'Light fixtures', decide which fixtures are appropriate for each location;
- referring to the section on 'Light levels', mark on the plan which levels are appropriate where.

This will give you a master plan that you can use to select and install lighting yourself, or to give to a contractor.

## Noise

Although you may regard your home as a peaceful place, noise can be a real problem for the home-worker. There are two elements to this noise:
- the noise you make;
- the noise around you.

If *you* make too much noise you may be forced to stop by your local authority, if they receive a complaint. Also if *others* make too much noise, it can affect your work. The kind of noise you experience working at home can be a real shock. There are two sides to this:
- you may be used to working in commercial premises which are noise insulated;
- you may never have been at home long enough to notice noise levels for a protracted period.

When you work from home, noises can come to the fore all of a sudden. And what is more, you will be hearing these day in, day out. Examples include:

- dogs;
- children and schools;
- road traffic, trains, aeroplanes;
- televisions, hi-fis;
- household noises.

Any of these can be very disruptive. One person we spoke to when writing this book decided to start working from home as a counsellor. In the past she had been used to going out to work, spending only a few hours at home in the evening. She soon found out that her neighbours liked to play loud pop music during the day. This background music hindered discussions with people about their personal problems, and made working from home rather difficult.

## Minimising noise

The key is to minimise the kind of noises that annoy you. You have a range of options which include:
- fitting secondary or double-glazing;
- adding some simple sound insulation;
- positioning desks and workspaces away from windows, and outside or party walls.

Some people have stuck egg boxes to the walls to keep the noise down! This is only really OK if you don't have high profile clients visiting. However, simple techniques can work and it pays to:
- put a rubber mat or a piece of carpet underlay under washing machines, refrigerators, speakers, etc. to reduce noise transmitted through vibration;

- position noise sources away from walls, so that their effect on neighbours and family is limited.

A local builder will be able to advise you on more sophisticated approaches, including a very effective form of party wall insulation – a new kind of plasterboard which includes a felt backing. This can simply be stuck to battens on the wall with a vibration strip incorporated to deaden the sound waves. There are also special floor treatments along the same lines that can be used to reduce noise from above (either people above you, or you above them).

## Negotiating on noise

In the end, it is better to live harmoniously together with family and neighbours, and noise is increasingly regarded as a source of pollution, particularly in urban areas. One of the main problems with noise is that it can upset the people you live with, or their noise may distress you. In this case fitting secondary glazing isn't likely to help. This is where negotiation is important, and particularly negotiating the kind of hours you work. You may find that, although you feel you should be working late into the night, this is actually unreasonable for the people in your own home. It's likely that you will need to be very disciplined, and make noise only when others are out.

## Ventilation

Noise and ventilation are linked. You may decide to open the windows in hot weather while working at home, and in doing so raise the noise to an unacceptable level. You may have to decide between working against the noise from a busy road, or sweltering in a cauldron of heat with the windows shut. Another problem is that sometimes a room at home can be either too hot, or too cold. There are a range of things you can do to improve ventilation, including:

• fitting extractor fans;
• using fans;
• using heaters when required;
• installing air conditioning.

These may seem unnecessary, but it's important to bear them in mind in your plan. However, don't rush into having air conditioning until you have survived one heatwave, so that you can be sure you really need it. If you find you do, don't skimp, because another sweltering hot summer, working from home, may be enough to drive you back to employment.

## Storage

Storage is the great bugbear of people working from home. It's also one of the things that people think least about. The reason for this is that when you are working in a traditional workspace, storage is usually taken care of. However, at home, you can quickly find yourself buried under a mountain of material with nowhere to put it. Essential material can end up in the cellar, or garage, only to find out that mice or damp have ruined it. So think carefully about storage.

## Principles of storage

When you are working for a larger organisation, you can usually keep anything that may come in handy. This isn't likely to be an option when you work from home. So be ruthless. Whenever you are tempted to keep something, think hard about whether you really need it.

'Never have in your houses anything you do not know to be useful or believe to be beautiful.'

*William Morris*

Also, think before you buy something for your business. Do you really need to buy it right away? Try taking a 'just in time' approach to stock holding. For instance, if you are working at home as a carpenter, leave the timber yard to store your stock, and come to an agreement where your timber is delivered the day before, or the morning that you need it.

This type of approach requires careful planning and a level of trust between you and your suppliers, but if you get it right you can cut down on storage at home. The same goes for stationery. There are plenty of companies that will do next-day delivery of envelopes, paper, etc.

You ought to have regular reviews of what you are storing. You may find that you can throw things away or store them in a less bulky format, e.g. keeping things on computer disk rather than paper. The best storage tool isn't a shelf or filing cabinet; it is your own mind, and the discipline that allows you to store just what you need, and the foresight to know what you can dispose of.

## Basic storage mechanisms

There is a whole range of straightforward storage options, including:

- shelves;
- archive boxes;
- the eaves space in a house;
- filing cabinets;
- a garage.

The most common method – a pile on the floor – is not recommended.

There is a range of other storage options which you can find in most good office equipment warehouses, and in many furniture shops. Large retailers such as IKEA are developing a range of specialist office equipment that can be used in the home as well. So keep your eyes open for new ideas.

## Equipment

One of the problems of working from home is that you can be lulled into a false sense of security. Nowhere is this more the case than when it comes to choosing equipment that will both:

- do the job, and
- keep you healthy and safe.

It is worth remembering the Frequency of Use principle here – the more you use a piece of equipment, the better it needs to be at doing the job, and keeping inherent risks to a minimum.

## Choosing the right equipment for the job

You really should spend time getting the best equipment you can afford. However, don't overdo things; sometimes a simple piece of equipment does the job, at half the cost. The secret is to buy items that are fit for the purpose you need them for.

Obviously, as you continue to work from home, your needs will become clearer, and you will add to the basic equipment that you buy. However, at the planning stage, you need to buy basic equipment that will last, will fit into your work space, and will function correctly.

## Different types of equipment

There are too many different items of equipment to look at in any detail in this book. Instead we look at some general rules concerning equipment purchase for home use:

- talk to people who are in a similar line of work about the equipment they bought. Their insight into what does and doesn't work can be invaluable;
- buy trade related magazines. These often include reviews of equipment for your chosen profession;
- buy the best you can afford. Don't overstretch yourself but always buy towards the top of your budget. There is no substitute for high quality equipment that will withstand wear and tear. Good quality, second-hand equipment may be cheaper, but bear in mind that it may no longer have guarantees or service agreements.

One of the problems of working from home is that you have little support. If you are running your own business from home, you need to have confidence in your equipment. Equipment that breaks down can lead to loss of work, and heartache. So do your research early and buy the best you can.

## Equipment for keeping in touch

These days there is no excuse for not being in touch with the outside world. Modern communication devices mean that you can be on call whenever you want to. Indeed this is one of the reasons why companies are increasingly asking employees to work from home. More and more, people are telling tales of woe about working from home, because they feel they never have any time to themselves.

You will need to decide just how much in touch you want to be quite early on, and plan your equipment accordingly.

In this section we will look at some basic office and communications equipment. Generally, the more in contact you are, the better. However, this will involve managing your time (see Chapter 5).

## Working out the costs

Before you start buying office or communications equipment work out what you can afford and what you want from it. Try using the 'pay back' exercise. If there is a piece of equipment you want, divide the cost of it over three years. Work out for each year whether you would spend more *without* the equipment than you would with it. If you would spend more, then it makes sense to buy or lease it.

Take the example of photocopying. In most workplaces these are taken for granted. When people begin working from home, they generally don't have a photocopier, which can be a real dilemma. Do you:

- spend the £300 upwards that a photocopier is going to cost, and budget for the running costs of paper, toner, electricity, etc.; or
- simply visit the local shop and purchase photocopies at 5p a sheet?

If you work out that the cost of buying and running a photocopier, is going to be less sheet-for-sheet, then you buy one. The hassle factor surrounding equipment should also be taken into account. If you have a pressing deadline you could probably do without dashing down the road to get one photocopy done.

You may decide to start simply. You can set up a home office with a PC, a printer, a telephone and an answer machine. You can add things such as fax machines later. Our advice is to buy good equipment but to start simple, if you can.

## Buying a computer

For many home businesses, this is likely to be the most important purchase you make. It can also be the most difficult, as there are so many computers on the market, and the market changes so rapidly. Buy a computer today and three months later it could well be obsolete. But don't let this put you off. If you need a computer now, buy one.

A strategy for buying:
- work out the maximum amount you can afford;
- clarify all your reasons for buying a computer, e.g. for business, for your childrens' education, etc.;
- find out the *minimum* specifications you will need for your specific purposes; then buy the highest spec' you can afford;
- be aware that 'upgrading' a computer (by adding extra features such as a CD-ROM drive, or more memory) is a more expensive way to buy, although it does spread the cost;
- list all the items you will need, including a printer, *Idiot's Guide*, etc.;
- work out costs by looking at one or two adverts in a computer magazine, and by asking in a few shops – then think again;
- ask to see demonstrations of software running on the computer. Go with a friend – they can take some pressure off you. Work out questions beforehand;
- size and design may be a factor. Feel comfortable with what you buy. The computer has to fit your workspace;
- be careful – VAT is rarely added to the display price of computers. Check out the level and cost of after-sales support. Consider extended warranty at the time of purchase;
- most people are mystified by computers so don't be afraid to ask for jargon-free explanations;
- write down the details of what you buy and what tasks it can perform, and get the salesperson to sign it.

## Telephones

Telephones are the life-blood of working from home. What we say about telephones may be out of date by the time you read this book, because the market is moving so fast. The best advice we can give you is to shop around, not to be seduced by the sales claims, and to be clear about the kind of system you *need*. Top-of-the-range telephones can:

- store hundreds of numbers and dial them up with a press of one button;
- act as a fax machine and modem;
- offer switching between different lines;
- allow you to move around with a handset linked by radio to your base unit;
- allow you to speak without having to hold the handset;
- offer dozens of other features.


You need to decide what your business *needs* and choose a telephone accordingly.

Consider these options:

- have a number of different lines on the same telephone number; this allows more than one person to pick up the phone up, or allows you to put an answer phone on one line, and your normal phone on the other. This means that people don't get the engaged signal constantly, if you are busy.
- add a second phone number; one for friends and relatives, the other for business; you could also run a fax machine or computer modem on the second line, without interrupting domestic calls.

*Mobile phones*

Again the market is changing quickly, and there is a vast range of options and tariffs available to you. Shop around and get a mobile phone that suits your *needs*. Many mobile phones include an answering service – a good way of keeping in touch while on the move. Use them judiciously though; they can prove very expensive.

# Other new technology

There is a whole range of equipment you can buy. This includes:

- video phones: this may be a good idea if you keep in regular touch with a customer, or if it saves you travel to two or three meetings a year;
- modems: a modem attached to a PC is a wonderful way of sending computer files to people through the telephone line. This can save a lot of time and money, and modems are relatively inexpensive. A modem gives you access to the Internet which is great for getting information. There are plenty of Internet-related books on the market;
- the fax: the fax has taken its place alongside the phone for people working from home. Like phones, there are many different types of fax, and you should choose one to suit your needs. One of the choices you will be faced with is whether to buy a standard fax machine or a plain-paper one. A plain-paper fax allows you to do away with those curly, flimsy pieces of fax paper. However they cost more. If you are going to be receiving lots of faxes, and filing them, then it's probably worth getting a plain-paper fax machine;

- software: there is a breathtaking array of computer software on the market and our advice is to choose a basic 'office suite' that will meet most of your needs. You can add new software programmes later. Never and in no circumstances consider bootlegging software packages. It is illegal and is unfair on the people who are making a living producing it;
- computer printers: there are hundreds on the market, and you will probably need to spend more money than you anticipate. Always buy the best printer you can afford. Test some of your own documents on printers, before you buy. You may be able to buy a printer on approval from one of the direct mailing organisations;
- photocopiers: we looked at photocopiers earlier (page 162). Photocopiers are capable of reduction, enlargement, and colour-copying, and vary in speed. But remember that what you *need* is often different to what you *want*; so stick with 'fitness for purpose'.

## Service agreements

Service agreements are a complex issue, and the problem is one of balancing probabilities. Many of the service agreements offered by shops selling office equipment are exorbitantly expensive. You may think that there is little point in having a service agreement, because equipment should last three years.

However, if a machine breaks down and you don't have a service agreement, it can cause you immense pain. It is always worth approaching the manufacturers direct to see what service and warranty agreements they offer. Often their agreements are much better value. Some stores, such as John Lewis, offer full, three year on-site warranties for all computer and office equipment.

## Selecting healthy and safe equipment

Most equipment and furniture in the home is designed for temporary or infrequent use. They are not designed for the rigours of work. At the planning stage, it is important to try to make your workspace as healthy as possible. Health and Safety is looked at in more detail in Chapter 2, but here we look at some of the issues surrounding the most common pieces of equipment that you are likely to need.

People who work from home often end up with occupational injuries caused by poor design of their workspace. One of the most common complaints is bad backs, from using inappropriate desks, and chairs.

*Some sources of advice*
The first important step is to get advice on purchasing equipment that will help you stay healthy. For instance:
• your GP;
• your local osteopath;
• HSE.

These people can provide you with helpful leaflets on the subject. Without going into great detail, here are some of the things that you should consider.

*The desk or workbench*
If your desk is too low or too high you will strain your back. It's possible to purchase adjustable desks where

you can alter the height to suit your body shape. If you can't afford an adjustable desk, try to adjust the level of your existing desk in some (safe) way.

*The chair*
For many people, working from home means spending longer hours sitting down. If this is the case, it is *well worth* investing in a chair that will support your back properly. A poor chair can also lead to neck problems, migraines and other associated risks.

*The computer*
You may do work that doesn't involve a computer, but this could soon change. It is essential to position a computer correctly. The screen should be at the same level as your head. You can buy support stands from specialist shops to rectify this, or use something sturdy from the home. Also, keep both your feet on the floor, and your elbows at a 90° bend.

## Appointing contractors
If your workspace needs any sort of structural or technical alteration that you cannot handle, you need to hire a contractor. When any contractor (or supplier) comes to discuss your working environment with you, remember that they have not had the benefit of the thought processes that led to your decision to make alterations. Also, he or she will:
• probably have different tastes, experiences and attitudes from your own;

- not know what is in your mind;
- need a very clear and precise explanation of what you
  want doing.

The consequences of misunderstandings and breakdowns
in communication over contractual work are obvious:
- people get upset;
- time wasted on recrimination, claim and counter-claim;
- hassles over payment that can end up in court.

You need to form a good relationship with your
contractors; the most creative and productive come about
if both parties collaborate towards a common goal. Good
contractors want to enhance their reputation by doing a
good job, just as you do when you work for others.

There will be some occasions where it will be in your
best interest to trust the expertise of a contractor, and
allow yourself to be guided by their judgement,
particularly at the design stage. Obviously there is a
degree of risk involved, but your chances of being
disappointed with the end result are narrowed if:
- you have done your homework and selected a sound
  contractor;
- you have seen examples of their previous work;
- the contractor's ideas are supported by drawings or
  plans that give a clear impression of what will be done;
- your instructions to them are crystal clear and specific
  in every detail.

Remember that the root cause of a problem could be *your*
instructions. If you are not sure that a contractor is clear

about what you want, or feel uneasy about working with them, look for another contractor. There should be somebody, somewhere with whom you will have a meeting of minds.

# Finding the right contractor

For each job, try to find at least three contractors to choose from. Do not:

• just open the Yellow Pages and stick in a pin;
• give the job straightaway, to someone you 'bump into';
• simply opt for the cheapest estimate you get.

Instead:

• ask around for recommendations:
– people you know who have had similar work done;
– contractors who have done work for you satisfactorily – they may have contacts, and will rarely put their own reputation on the line by giving you a bad lead;
• contact accredited trade bodies for a list of members.

When you have narrowed the field down to three, ask the contractors for the following:

• how long they have been in business?
• how long have they been at their current address?
• can they provide references?
• do they have a portfolio that you can see?
• can they show you some of their work?
• are they registered for VAT?
• are they part of a trade association that offers indemnity against possible problems (e.g. if the contractor goes out of business)? Be specific about this, as there are many trade associations that don't offer insurance guarantees.

- do they have public liability insurance, and can they show you the certificate?

If they cannot provide enough information to give you confidence in them, or they hedge with their answers, reject them.

In some cases, particularly for large contracts, it may be worth checking the contractor's *Annual Report and Returns* at Companies House. This information should give you an idea of how safe financially it is to deal with the company. This information is only available for limited companies.

*Key points to watch*
Hiring contractors can be stressful, but the following check list should help you get things right:

- personal recommendations are best.
- check that the firm belongs to a trade association and that membership really does act as a guarantee.
- try to avoid having work done in emergency. It causes a lot of pressure and gives you less room to haggle with a contractor. If they know something is an emergency, they can charge more.
- you can negotiate better prices with a contractor during quiet periods in the trade. Quiet periods include late autumn, and winter, particularly around Christmas.
- the Office of Fair Trading advises consumers to short list three or four contractors and then invite offers. Draw up a job specification and make it absolutely clear what you want. State that you want a firm price, not an estimate.

171

- be absolutely clear about the time when you want the job done. If the contractor can't offer you a start and finish date, either ask for a reduction or find someone else.
- don't go for a quote that is too cheap. If a company quotes too cheap, the chances are they will add to the price later, or do a shoddy job.
- don't be shy about telling the contractor their price is too high.
- quality of work and price are inter-related. You want the work to be done well, because you want it to last.
- don't pay any money in advance. You may agree to staged payment, but wait until the work is completed, until you pay the bulk. For work over £5 000 you should give the builder a contract, and make them sign it. The Royal Institute of Chartered Surveyors provides template contracts for you to work from.

## Specifying your requirements

You should meet with your chosen contractor to clarify what will be done, for how much and by when. Prepare everything you need, before the meeting, so that you give a clear message to the contractor. For the meeting, sit at a table, so that you can spread out all the information you both need to look at.

You will need the following:
- drawing pad, pencil and rubber;
- five or more photocopies of your plans and drawings;
- two copies of the job specification (one for the contractor).

Be very specific and detailed about what you tell the

contractor to quote for. Explain:
- what result you want to see;
- why it matters;
- what background planning you have done yourself;
- what exactly you want them to do.

At the end of the meeting the contractor should be prepared to submit a quotation to you.

## Quotations and estimates

There is a big difference between an estimate and a quotation. An estimate is only an educated guess at what the final invoice might be. A quotation states exactly what you will pay. There are times when it is not possible for a contractor to be certain about prices, e.g. it is difficult to assess the condition of a flooring joist until the floor has been taken up. In these instances, tell the contractor that you expect a separate, written quotation, before you agree to any additional work being done.

Ask for a detailed, written quotation for all work and make sure that it is signed. A proper quotation will take a day or two, so expect to wait. Check the quotation against your specification to make sure that everything that you asked for is included. Never assume something is included, if it is not in the quotation. If something has been missed out ask for the quotation to be rewritten.

*VAT*

Make sure that all quotations clearly state whether VAT is included or not. Some companies include the VAT amount in the figures, others simply state that VAT is not included. This is a good reason for not accepting verbal quotations. You will find yourself in a very difficult position, if you are told at the end of a job that the quotation didn't include VAT.

Avoid contractors who reduce prices for cash or say they can remove the VAT if you keep things informal. It is reasonable to assume that they are not operating ethically, and if they are avoiding responsibility in this area, they might avoid it elsewhere. Also, they will probably not issue proper receipts in this instance, which will:

- prevent you from claiming the expense against your business;
- adversely affect your case if you enter into a legal dispute with them;
- put you at risk if the Inland Revenue investigates.

*Payment terms*
Establishing payment terms is critical, not just because it can affect the job, but also because it will affect your cashflow (page 100). Surprise demands for payment can ruin plans to pay important suppliers. Make sure that the quotation clearly states when payments are to be made, whether initial payments for materials, or final payment. Always hold back a significant proportion of the total payment, until you are satisfied the job has been completed. Asking a contractor back to do remedial work will be very difficult otherwise.

Remember that payment terms are for you to decide, not the contractor. If the terms do not suit you, do not accept them. If at any stage the contractor demands unscheduled payments, do not pay. If you are unsure of your rights, contact a solicitor before paying.

*Deadlines*
If it is important for you to know when the job starts and/or finishes, get a written commitment from the contractor stating that all deadlines will be met. It may be appropriate to include penalty clauses, in the case the work is not completed on time. This can mean that after an agreed completion date, for each day or week that the job runs over, a specified amount is deducted from the final bill.

For costly, or very involved work, it is worth getting a solicitor to check agreements before you enter into them. The Citizens Advice Bureau can give advice, if you cannot afford a solicitor. You will find their number in your local telephone directory.

*Terms and Conditions*
Most quotations will have these, very often in small print on the back. Do not overlook them. If there is anything you are not happy with, refer it to a solicitor, or the Citizens Advice Bureau.

*During the job*
The presence of strangers in your home, carrying out noisy and/or messy jobs can be very disruptive and stressful, particularly if you are trying to work in the middle of it all. Relationships with contractors can easily become strained, and your patience may run out. If you find yourself at the point of confronting a worker, do take

a second to remember some important factors:
- the reason for your grumpiness may be less to do with the contractor, and more to do with you having a bad day;
- it is often difficult for a contractor to carry out their work *without* causing some inconvenience;
- losing your temper will not help things at all;
- think about how your commitment to providing a good service is affected if a customer does not appear to appreciate your efforts. If you treat someone with respect, they are more likely to do a good job for you.

# 5 DEVELOPING A SUCCESSFUL APPROACH TO WORK

The previous chapters looked at issues you need to consider *before* starting to work from home. When you are up and running there are some key actions and approaches that will help you build on your preparation, and to work from home successfully. We explore tactics and techniques for staying in control – both of your business and your personal life.

First, we take a brief look at the image you present with your stationery, and ways of promoting yourself to potential customers.

## Stationery

The image you convey is everything – and first impressions count. Often the first point of contact you have with a potential client is through your letterhead and/or business card. So they need to make a positive statement about you and your business. Sit down and think carefully about the image you want to convey, and the types of communications you will make.

### Letterhead design

Image is everything, but the kind of image will vary according to the nature of the business, e.g. a designer may want to convey creativity, but a plumber may wish to appear swift and efficient. However, there is one common theme – to make people want to do business with you. So how do you gain their attention?

A good starting point is to think about letterhead design. There are three main elements of a letterhead:
- whether or not to use a logo;
- the overall appearance (typeface, design, etc.);
- colour.

*Do you need a logo?*
Any new business needs to get noticed, and a logo can be very effective for this. People recall images more easily than words. The advertising industry spends billions of pounds developing instantly recognisable logos that become synonymous with products. A logo can be:
- a stylised version of a company name or initials;
- a name and image combined, e.g. Lloyds Bank and the Black Horse, Apple computers;
- an image that comes to signify the company or product, e.g. the Dulux dog, Comic Relief's red nose.

If you decide to create a logo try not to be too clever. No logo is generally preferable to one that looks amateurish. In any case you can always get it professionally designed later.

*Questions to ask yourself*
Try answering the following questions to help you decide on an appropriate logo:
- can you do anything with your own/company initials to create a logo, e.g. create a monogram, spell a word?
- is there an image or object that encapsulates what you do, e.g. a padlock for a security firm?
- does your/company name bring any images to mind,

e.g. a bridge for D. Bridges?
- does the place you work have a particular image that says something positive about your work – for instance, City Trading, Bond Street Gems or Country Crafts?

*Feedback*
Get a range of friends (and if possible potential customers) to give you their honest opinion. If nothing seems to work, stick with your name only.

*Reproducing a logo*
You may want to reproduce your logo on a computer. To transfer an image to a computer you need a scanner. Your local copy shop may be able to scan your logo for you.

# Legal requirements
There is a legal requirement to include some information on your stationery. For a sole trader or partnership you have to include the name of the firm, if it is different from that of the owner. Also, for partnerships, include the names of all the partners.

A limited company's stationery must show:
- the full registered name of the company;
- the registration number and where it is registered;
- a clear statement of the address of the registered office, in addition to any other addresses such as the one from which a letter comes.

Anyone sending out an invoice, or quoting for a job, that includes a VAT element must quote their VAT registration number. The easiest thing to do is include your VAT registration number on every piece of stationery.

*Good practice*
The law aside, there are sound business reasons for including certain information on correspondence. Obvious things to include on letterheads are:
• your company name and address;
• telephone, fax number; e-mail address;
• VAT registration number;
• maybe a 'strap line' or slogan;
• possibly your own name, if you are the sole contact.

If you are not a limited company, you can limit what you put on compliments slips to a more succinct version of the full details. On your business card put:
• your name;
• a business title;
• any *relevant* qualifications, i.e. professional
  qualifications, City & Guilds etc.
• your contact address and telephone number(s).

## Overall appearance of print
Keep things clear and simple. Don't try to cram in too much information.

*Typeface*
There is a huge range of typefaces (fonts) to choose from, and the choice is often down to personal preference. There are a couple of points worth noting:
• if you use one of the standard fonts on most word

processors or desktop publishing systems, it could save you time finding a printer or designer to do extra design work for you later;

- use a sensible font size – small print can be difficult to read. Check people can read your stationery. As a guide, this book uses 10.5 point Times for the main text, and 10.5 to 17 point type for the headings;
- avoid using too many font sizes on your stationery – it confuses the eye;
- think very carefully before choosing a script font – one that imitates handwriting. Very few people prefer these to standard fonts, and some people regard them as frivolous.

*Layout*

Again, there are no hard and fast rules. Put the most useful information, such as your address and telephone number, somewhere prominent. Things like company registration number, and VAT number can be put near the foot of the paper.

*Colour*

Clever use of colour can make your stationery stand out. Imagine a desk covered in paperwork; you should aim to make it stand out and say 'read me now!'

Some colours are more easily noticed. Walk into a room and you are likely to register colours in the order: reds, bright blues, greens or yellows – then the rest. But remember that colours can suggest different things. Deep blues and reds can look very classy; neutral beiges or greens may suggest environmental concerns; neon

colours suggest something more upbeat.
Printing in more than one colour can get expensive, but
you can get round this by:
• printing onto coloured paper;
• printing in only blue for example, instead of using
  black.
Beware of headache-inducing colours such as red.

*Photographs*
These can be expensive to reproduce, but may be
worthwhile, if you are an actor, model, or artist. Artists
sometimes choose to use a picture to illustrate their work.
   Colour photocopies can be a cheaper option, but the
quality varies greatly, and probably isn't good enough for
letterheads.

## Comparing stationery designs
Gather together a range of letterheads and business cards.
Line them up on a table and see which ones stand out.
Then ask yourself *why* they stand out, and use the same
ideas.

## Where can you get a design?
You can either:
• use a professional designer;
• take one 'off the shelf';
• do one yourself.

*Using a designer*
Employing a professional designer or design agency can
be very expensive – so you may want to save your money

until you are more established. That said, if you know of a reputable, smaller agency (especially one trying to establish its own business) you may get a better deal. Make sure that you:

- explain you have a fixed budget;
- ask them what they can do for the price;
- will have the right to use the design they produce.

The best way to find a good designer is by personal recommendation. Otherwise, find material produced for another small business you like. You may find the designer's name on the material; if not phone the company and ask them for the name. If all else fails, look in Yellow Pages. Use the same sorts of checks to select a designer as you would any other contractor (page 168)

*Off the shelf*
Some printing firms and office suppliers have pattern books of standard format designs which you can pick and adapt. If you are hopeless at design this may be a good alternative. The downside is that your design may look similar to someone else's.

*DIY*
Think carefully before doing your own design, if you are not a designer. If you do decide to design things yourself, keep it simple, and remember these points:

- the more colours you use the more expensive it will be to print;
- photos are far more expensive to reproduce than simple line drawings;

- stay relevant – the logo should add something, not confuse people about what you do;
- don't be tempted to 'borrow' or copy a design without first asking permission.

A certain Mr Harrod marginally adapted the lettering style used by the famous Knightsbridge store for his hardware shop, and ended up in court for what he thought was 'a little joke'.

## Useful tools for design work

- computer software: allows you to position blocks of text on screen, wherever you want. Many computers come with drawing software, and icons which you can reproduce. You may need to check the copyright first. Professional desktop publishing software will allow you to produce higher quality designs.
- Letraset™: rub-on lettering that comes in a huge range of typefaces (fonts).
- photocopier: blow-up and reduce your designs to see how effective they look at different sizes. You can also mock-up letterheads, business cards or presentation folders.
- typewriter correction fluid: handy for correcting mistakes in drafts – but avoid using the fluid on finished copies.
- Spray mount: special spray-on fixative which allows you to stick down, peel off and re-position paper. Available from art shops and larger stationers.

# Other printed material

Letterhead design is a starting point, but you may also need to include your name/logo on other stationery and objects; for example:

- faxes;
- labels for envelopes, parcels and computer disks;
- folders, bags, other printed containers;
- product labels, from stick-on or tie-on labels for containers or objects, to sew-in textile tags and indelible ink stamps;
- banners, posters, trading signs, exhibitions, etc.;
- car stickers – a transfer or magnetic poster stuck to a car door can provide useful advertising.

Think about how your design will look in *all* the formats you will need.

# Dealing with the printer

When you have decided on a design, and the sort of stationery you want, you will need to get it printed. Printing is largely common sense, but you may find some of the terminology confusing. Here is a brief glossary:

*Typefaces and sizes*
- Font: the typeface design. Common fonts are Palatino, Times, Helvetica and Univers.
- Point: a measure of type (font) size. The larger this is, the larger the font. There are 72 points to an inch.

*Paper: sizes and quantities*
The standard file size is A4 – the size of a student pad

you can get at a stationers. A3 is double the size of A4, A2 is double A3, and A1 is double A2. A5 is half A4, and so on. A ream of paper is 500 sheets.

*Types of paper*
Coated/Matt/Gloss refers to the surface treatment of the paper (just like photos). Coated paper gives a tougher finish, but it can change the appearance of blocks of colour.

*Weight of paper*
Measured in grams per square metre (gsm). This indicates the weight, and hence the thickness of a piece of paper. The larger the gsm, the thicker the paper:
• photocopier paper is generally 80 gsm;
• most letters are written on 90 or 100 gsm;
• 150gsm is fairly thick card.

*Paper surfaces*
'Wove' is flat finished paper, and 'laid' is the sort of grained effect that can look rather upmarket. Laid, however, can be hard to print on, especially on photocopiers and computer printers.

*Colour printing*
Full- or four-colour printing gives a photographic level of colour representation. Four standard colours are each overprinted on one another to produce a picture.

Two-colour printing usually involves the use of separate blocks of colour (e.g. some red areas and some blue), though it can include combinations of the two colours, and tints as well. In printing, black is a colour, so two-colour printing can be black plus one other colour.

*Pantone*$^{TM}$
A reference number that identifies a colour precisely in an industry-standard (Pantone$^{TM}$) colour chart.

## Promoting your business

However good you are at what you do, the success of any business depends on customers knowing about you. This means that you need to get your name and details across to potential customers. There are many ways to promote yourself and your services or goods.

## Cold calling

Cold calling is contacting someone, either by telephone or in person, without an appointment. This can be a nightmare or a joy, depending on the person making (and receiving) the calls. We call this approach a promotional activity, because you are very unlikely to make a sale on the first call.

Cold callers are turned away time after time, but even if you get a 'no', make sure that you get at least some useful information, e.g. about what the firm buys, how often, and where from. Secretaries, receptionists and clerical staff are excellent sources of information. Try to use new information to convince people later, that you have something that may be of interest to them, i.e. link cold calls with some *positive* promotion, like:
• dropping off your price list or brochure;

- following up telephone calls with a brochure addressed
to the buyer, whose name you got when you rang.

This way a potential customer as least knows that you
exist. Don't apologise about what you are selling
– always be positive. If you are not positive, the customer
won't be!

## Promotion tactics

To get your name and business ideas into potential
customers' minds (and keep it there), you could do one or
more of a range of things:
- advertise on your car – but check with the insurance
company first;
- advertise in the local press, if you are aiming at a local
market;
- target specialist journals and magazines;
- hold a stand at exhibitions and conferences;
- distribute leaflets; remember to make leaflets striking –
people tend to throw 'junk mail' in the bin;
- stick leaflets under windscreen wipers – but beware of
the litter implications;
- advertise on local radio, this can be a lot cheaper than
you think;
- go out of your way to socialise with possible clients.
And some rather more imaginative approaches ...
- do a press release for the local paper or a specialist
magazine – they are always on the lookout for good
copy and unusual stories; an article is free advertising;
- enter a national competition; a man who came second
on the BBC's *Masterchef* found his business suddenly

took off. The man now runs a highly successful
enterprise, and makes regular TV appearances;
- offer to give lectures or demonstrations on what you
  do. For example, people selling dried flowers often
  provide free talks to groups and clubs, as this generates
  sales and gets them known;
- do the odd publicity stunt – something to catch the
  public imagination, but that doesn't rebound and give
  you a bad name;
- sponsor a local group to get your name known.

## Staying in control of your work

You should expect to be busy when you start working
from home. There will be a lot of things to do and set up.
With a business the aim is to get orders from day one, but
sometimes success brings its own problems, as a heavy
workload can increase general pressures.

You must control the business side of things, and to do
this you have to know what is happening and take active
management decisions. It is vitally important that you see
yourself as a manager. There may be no-one else to
manage, but you still have to manage aspects of the
business. Avoid one of the most common pitfalls –
thinking that being busy is the same as being productive,
or that being *efficient* is the same as being *effective*.

*Efficiency and effectiveness*

These are different concepts. You can be very efficient
without being at all effective. Efficiency is doing things
right. Effectiveness is doing the right things. You can do
all the wrong things to a very high standard, and your

business will fail. On the other hand you can do the right things, less well and still achieve success.

A prime example of an area where working from home can lead to efficiency at the expense of effectiveness is when pressures from the business make you react to external pressures rather than take control.

## Active and reactive management

Reactive managers are so busy with the tasks in hand, that they rarely take time to stop and consider what they *ought* to be doing. By responding to the latest crisis, or the most recent order, they leave no time to prioritise or plan for the future. As soon as this happens the business is controlling you, rather than you controlling the business. This can quickly lead to failure.

Successful managers use an *active* approach that puts them in the driving seat. They:

• manage the whole business rather than focusing only on certain aspects;
• know where they are in relation to earlier forecasts and plans;
• make decisions that take operations forward.

You must take an active management approach. This helps you to revise your plans, and stay in control.

View your work or business as a journey. Your original plans are a route map setting out the way forward. But not all journeys go according to plan. It is common for people to find that they are not where they expected to be at a given time. There could be delays along the way, or you may reach a point ahead of schedule, or take a wrong turn. It is madness not to stop and take stock, and make further plans to complete your trip. Build regular reviews into your schedules, so that you know whether things are on track or not.

*Monitoring and reviewing*
Monitoring and reviewing are different activities.
Monitoring:
- checks progress in a specific issue or activity against set criteria;
- is current, as the event takes place;
- is basically an early warning system;
- provides a means of collecting information over time that can be used in a wider review.

Reviewing:
- looks back to see what happened and why;
- provides a chance to consider the evidence and decide whether to take corrective action.

*Monitoring*
Monitoring means setting up criteria for specific measures or events, and using them as a form of early warning. The bank monitors your account by comparing your balance against set limits every day. If you go over the limit, you get a call or a letter. A heart monitor checks your heartbeat.

For you, working from home, the areas you need to monitor depend on the nature of your work, but they often include:
- the number of orders taken daily;
- cashflow (page 100);

191

- where you stand with orders that are due to be completed;
- the state of the order book for the immediate and longer term future.

These are all essentially statistical areas, where you can measure fairly accurately whether or not the situation is within acceptable limits. To measure anything you have to identify specific criteria as yardsticks or benchmarks, for example:

- how many orders do you want to take daily?
- when should you finish a job, or, how much progress should be made in a day?
- how many orders do you need to maintain a safe buffer for the future?

As well as the alarm bell factor, information gathered during monitoring is invaluable when you come to do a business review.

*Reviews*
You should plan to hold regular reviews to look at:
- what has happened over a given period;
- what was expected to happen;
- where there are any variances;
- why they occurred;
- what this tells you;
- whether there is a need to make other plans.

The danger of *reacting* instead of *reviewing* is that you miss obvious things. When you are busy, it is remarkably easy to miss sensible courses of action. The following is based on a true story, although the exact details have been changed.

---

**Selling your way into trouble**

A supplier of car alarms was always busy, so it came as a shock when the bank expressed concern about the business.

Immediately, the supplier sprang into action, advertising and promoting his products at a discount. Sales almost doubled. The owner was delighted … and the business went broke.

---

The mistake was the reaction to sell more. The supplier was an excellent salesman, but he had not reviewed *profit* levels for some time. There had been several small increases in raw materials, and to remain competitive the owner pegged his prices. In other words, the costs had gone up, but the revenue had not. The costs in fact, exceeded income, so each car alarm made a loss. By selling more, the owner made the problem worse. By discounting prices he added even more fuel to the fire.

Reviewing costs, sales margins and the business *overall* would have given the business owner the information needed to make a sensible decision

*The need for regular reviews*
Work reviews are like health check-ups. They are not nearly as effective, if you wait until there is a problem. Given the pressures that develop when working from home, it is important to:
• decide on a schedule for reviews – maybe monthly to

begin with, and quarterly as things settle down;
• specify what will be reviewed – which information will be analysed.

In addition to regular interim reviews, the information gathered and the decisions taken during the year help revise your business plan.

*Annual revision of business plans*
It is important to take an annual look at your business, against the most recent business plan – which should be the one for your current year. Everyone who starts a business should make a business plan, especially if they want support from a bank. However, very few people ever look at it again. This is not only a missed opportunity – it is dangerous.

The initial business plan can only be a series of assumptions, best guesses and projections. The business has not started, so the business plan is more of an art than a science. The most common complaint from individuals doing their initial business plan is that they can't do it – usually because they haven't tried! These are frequently the same people who fail to revise their business plan, even though revised plans deal with real evidence and experience.

Collecting information is relatively straightforward, but interpreting it can be difficult. There is a powerful technique that can help.

# Pareto analysis
The Pareto principle (or the 80:20 rule) is remarkably

effective. Its main characteristics are:
- it is relatively simple to do;
- it highlights priority areas for action, helping you to tackle important issues first;
- it is remarkably informative and accurate;
- what it tells you, is often quite surprising.

The basis of the approach is that 80% of something is driven by or results from 20% of something else. It does not matter what – it could be that:
- 80% of telephone calls come in a period that is 20% of the day;
- 80% of delivery costs are spent on deliveries to 20% of an area;
- 20% of customers cause 80% of the problems;
- 80% of breakdowns are on 20% of machines;
- 20% of sales calls are on restaurants and they result in 80% of the business.

The main benefit of identifying such patterns is that it allows you to tackle priority areas. With limited resources it is sensible to spend them wisely.
For the previous patterns:
- you could work on problem issues and raise the profile of successful areas;
- you could target the servicing of the 20% of machines that cause most of the problems;
- you could plan a sales campaign to restaurants – when you have identified with market research what it is that the restaurants find so attractive about your product or service.

You could even decide to stop doing business with some or all of the 20% of troublesome customers. You may spend so much time and money servicing them that they cost you money. The time might be better spent developing more satisfactory, and profitable business relationships.

## Step-by-step guide to Pareto analysis

*Step 1*
Decide what it is you want to measure. You could usefully look at:
- which products or services are most popular;
- which provide the best profit margins;
- where most of your costs are incurred;
- which geographical areas have been the source of most business;
- which advertising and promotion has brought the best results;
- who are your bad payers;
- which customers give you the most problems.

*Step 2*
Collect data from your records. This is where monitoring can make the process easier. Decide from the outset to monitor the areas in Step 1. Keep running records for review dates.

*Step 3*
Analyse the results. The results may not break down into 80 and 20. They could be 70:30 or even 60:40, but you

will see patterns emerging. You could find for example that:

- the majority of orders come from a smallish number of customers;
- most of your orders are from one part of the range (if you offer a range);
- the bulk of your turnover comes from a small number of products;
- the majority of your costs arise from a small number of activities;
- most of your profit comes from a few products – although they may be different products from those providing the turnover;
- a few customers are responsible for nearly all late payments.

*Step 4*
Take decisions based on your results. This is a matter of *judgement* rather than statistical analysis. For example, you may find that some products or services make no profit. However, you may choose not to drop unprofitable areas, because 80% of your more profitable work comes from the 20% of customers who originally bought your unprofitable products.

On the other hand, if 20% of your supplies account for 80% of raw material costs, it should prompt you to look for more competitive suppliers, or cheaper alternatives.

*Step 5*
Finally, check your results against your business plan to see how accurate your previous forecasts were. You can

use this to make your next plan more realistic.

The long-term results of this exercise can be extremely positive. By monitoring and reviewing regularly, and using analytical techniques, you can sharpen up your approach and control costs, customers and products to maximise profits, and reduce waste.

## Staying in control of your life

This may sound melodramatic, but anyone who has worked from home will testify that it eats into your time and your energy. You must take action to stay healthy, stress-free and in control of your time. All these are much easier said than done. There are three main areas to look at here:

- making the most of your time;
- handling stress and having a life away from work;
- developing an assertive approach for resisting unacceptable pressures, and finding workable agreements with customers.

## Making the most of your time

Time management is one of the main difficulties for people in today's world. The bottom line is that there are 168 hours in a week. You are the only person who can sort out how you spend (or waste) it. This does not mean filling it all with work. Instead, it means making rules and conventions to stick to, so that you remain in control of your time. The following are the key elements in successful time management.

*Spend time planning and managing time*

Time management is an active management process. The underlying principle of time management is that you must invest a few minutes each day reviewing and planning your activities. The day may turn out to be different to what you expected, but planning increases your level of control.

Time spent on time management is an investment, not a cost. It pays dividends. So make the commitment now – decide to take control and invest a few minutes each day to save hours later.

*Decide what matters*

In a business, the first critical factors are your key aims and goals. An employee's goals are linked directly to the purpose of their job. If you are self-employed, your goals are likely to be:

- building a successful business;
- having a sense of achievement;
- earning a certain level of income;
- building excellent relationships with customers;
- increasing the number of customers;
- achieving a certain turnover.

There are others, but the above are fairly common. The key point is that all your work hours should be related to your key aims and goals. Unless you have time to spare, the priority is to do things that bring you closer to your goals. This sounds easy enough, but there are certain problems. Do you recognise yourself in any of the following?

199

- prefer to do less vital things, and spend more time on them than they merit – everyone dislikes doing some things, but you need to tackle crucial tasks, however distasteful;
- don't let go of tasks that you enjoy, even if they are unproductive and someone else could do them – consider whether you can achieve more by leaving tasks you do to others, e.g. calling on the services of an accountant, builder or secretary.;
- lose sight of the goals – when pressure builds up, trivial problems can assume disproportionate dimensions; keep things in proportion and cancel that visit by the sales representative.

## Check what happens now

For a reasonable period – say a couple of weeks – keep a detailed record of *everything* you do, right down to the last telephone call, coffee, tidying up session ... whatever. Keep a diary for each day, split up into half-hour blocks. In each block note down everything you do. Note down the following information for each activity:

- what the activity was;
- how long you spent on it;
- whether it took you any closer to your goals;
- whether it was productive;
- whether you had planned to do it or it was unplanned.

This takes time, but the results can often pay huge dividends. Analyse the time you spent on activities by using the headings above, and grouping things together. Common patterns are:

- things you thought took only a few minutes take a lot longer;
- spending time on non-productive (but often enjoyable)tasks while productive ones sat waiting;
- going back over the same ground – maybe making two deliveries when one trip would have saved time;
- spending more time on unplanned activity than planned – reacting to other people's demands rather than trying to achieve your goals.

By thinking through the implications of your results you can immediately make some adjustments to your work patterns, and save time. There will be some activities – maybe a lot – that were unplanned. That's life; you cannot plan every minute of every day. But if you know how much time is spent generally on that unplanned activity, you can start to allow for it.

## Sort out urgent and important tasks

This is central to effective time management. Urgent tasks are not the same as important ones.

*Urgency*
Urgent tasks are often trivial and of little value. They tend to be generated by other people and are reactive. Examples include:

- responding to a telephone call from a sales rep who has asked you to ring them back urgently; although you know it is routine;
- filling in forms that someone else wants you to complete, when they are of no real use to you;

• tidying up.

Urgent tasks have to be done, but they do not generally relate to the goals.

*Importance*
Important tasks relate to goals. They are generally activities that you generate, to reach your goals. They are not often urgent, because important activities are usually planned. Examples include:
• doing the accounts;
• producing a new leaflet or brochure;
• reviewing the business and planning ahead;
• ringing customers to keep in touch.

Important activities have to be done, but they often get left until the last minute when urgent activities squeeze them out. Then they get rushed.

*Handling urgent and important tasks*
Be ruthless about sorting out what is urgent and what is important. Something may be important to someone else, but not to you. When you do urgent activities, do them quickly, and get them out of the way.

With important activities, remember that they are about your goals. Spend more time on them – by planning ahead and scheduling them in your diary if necessary. Remember, not everything has to be reactive and done by lunch time. Some things are urgent as well as important. If they are, do them immediately, but give them the time they deserve. If something is neither urgent nor important, do you need to do it?

## Schedule activities

*Make a list*
This is simple – but it needs discipline. Start every day
by making a list of everything you know you *have* to do.
Don't try and sort it out – just list things. Include
everything, whether it is urgent, important or both.

*Prioritise*
Sort the activities into urgent and important. Write down
an 'I' or a 'U' (or both) beside each task. You can deal
with the urgent ones quickly, in one block. Remember to
dump any that are neither important nor urgent. Then sort
the activities into groups. It doesn't matter how you do
this, but a couple of tried and tested approaches are:
A = high priority;
B = medium priority;
C = low priority.
or
• must be done today;
• should be done today;
• could be done today.

*Decide what action to take*
For each prioritised activity, consider whether to:
• bin it;
• give it to someone else to do;
• make a quick phone call or some other sort of a holding
  device, to buy yourself more time;
• do it yourself, today;
• do it yourself, another day.

*Timetable the activities*

Use a system for scheduling that suits you. Some people like a filofax; others use a year planner, wall chart, computer software, etc.. The important thing is to identify future commitments.

Allocate a time for each activity you have decided to do. **Do not underestimate.** If you think a trip to the bank manager will take an hour to prepare for, and an hour to sit through, don't forget the half-hour's travel. Allow three hours – things always take longer than you expect.

Delay some important things until the next day, the next week, or even next month. If they are not urgent, leave them – but plan them into your schedule. If the accounts are due at the end of next month, they are important but not urgent. Block out a whole day, next month, when things look less busy… and stick to it!

Some important points to remember:

- if something was Priority A at 9 o'clock, it remains priority A. Don't try and kid yourself that it has dropped down the scale, later in the day;
- giving a job to someone else or performing a holding operation both take time, so allow for it;
- build in time for the unexpected; the results of your diary analysis will show unplanned activity, and this will happen again;
- if things change during the day, go back and reschedule the whole day. Don't just forget your priorities, and start reacting to the day's events;
- allow more time for activities than you expect. It is never wasted, because if you finish something early, you can bring forward other tasks.

- If you put things off until later, it should be for a good reason, and not a cop-out; stick to things once they are scheduled.

*Work your way through*
Follow the plan you make at the start of the day, but try to follow these principles:
- wherever possible get rid of a lot of urgent and trivial tasks at the start of the day. Ticking off several 'things to do' in one go is a boost;
- if a crisis occurs, deal with it – but decide on its priority first;
- do things in blocks:
- making six or seven telephone calls together means you don't have to keep switching in and out of 'telephone mode';
- plan journeys – if you are going somewhere later in the week, ask yourself if you really have to go there today as well; you could telephone and save an extra trip;
- put days aside for key activities, e.g. try to do all your calls and deliveries on set days, rather than whenever someone rings up; it makes each day easier to manage and helps with scheduling;
- allow time for the unexpected.

*Make another list*
At the end of each day make a list of all the activities that will be on the next day's list. This achieves three things:
- it ensures you forget nothing;
- it saves you time in the morning;
- you end the day knowing you have done something

about everything on the morning's list – even if it is to plan it ahead for another day. This helps you relax and switch off.

## Handling stress

Stress has a bad name. It has almost become accepted that any stress is bad. This is not the case. It is *too much* stress that's the problem. Time management (page 198) is an excellent first step in stress control.

There is a certain level of stress below which it is extremely hard to get motivated. Having too little to do can be just as stressful as having too much. Everyone has their own optimal level of stress. Some people thrive on a high degree of pressure, while others are quite happy to lead a hassle-free life. Stress can be a particularly serious problem for people working from home. This is because work and relaxation are now under the same roof.

## Basic stress management

The common factors in limiting and reducing stress are linked to lifestyle. It is vital that you not only look after yourself while you work, but that you also have a life outside working from home. There are no 'quick fixes' that can remove stress. The key issues are that you must:

- get enough sleep;
- spend time on leisure pursuits, to balance your work activities;
- learn to relax;
- take regular exercise;
- eat sensibly and watch your diet – the psychological implications of being overweight can induce stress;

- avoid or cut down on drugs that increase stress –
  especially nicotine and caffeine; the idea that a coffee
  and a cigarette are good for the nerves is a popular
  misconception – they raise stress levels;
- take breaks during the day.

It also helps if you can maintain a healthy view of the
world, and keep things in perspective – something on the
lines of 'there will be days when I can sit in the sun and
relax'.

*Stress and working from home*
Controlling stress when you work from home can be very
hard. If you have too much to do, stress builds up.
Equally, if you have too little to do, inactivity and the fear
of failure can cause stress. You should try to do all or
most of the following:

- have a routine that matches one that someone at work
  would have. Your hours may be longer, but try to set
  yourself daily start and finish times, and *stick to them.*
  Enter repeat activities (e.g. deliveries, quarterly
  accounts) into your diary or schedule;
- keep promises about social and family activities. View
  them as important. Don't add to your stress by causing
  bad feeling at home, e.g. declining a family gathering,
  to do invoices;
- avoid 'contaminating' some days. If you are having a
  complete day off… make it complete. **Do not** succumb
  to temptation and 'just do half-an-hour'. Your batteries
  recharge better, if you take a complete break;
- get a 'closed' sign. Even if you work alone – at the end

of the day, put up this physical reminder to stay away;
- buy an answering machine. You could spend whole evenings answering work calls that frankly could wait until the next day. If you are accessible the calls will continue, and probably escalate; let people know when you are not available. This way they will start to plan accordingly.

## Being assertive

Assertiveness helps you stay in control as you work to find a compromise that suits everyone, including you. Assertiveness is not the same as being aggressive, which is about threatening, bullying or devious behaviour. Assertiveness respects the rights of other people to have an opinion, a view or a set of feelings. However, it does not mean 'giving in' to keep the peace in the short term, and then failing to deliver, or feeling like a victim later – that's passive behaviour.

There are many excellent books written on assertiveness (e.g. *Putting Assertiveness to Work*, Willcocks and Morris, Pitman, 1996.). It is possible here only to scratch the surface, and give you the key points. Assertiveness is about three key factors:
- listening to the other person and recognising their point of view;
- having the right to say what your point of view is;
- finding common ground that can lead to a workable compromise.

If any of these factors is missing, you are not being assertive. Not listening to the other person is aggressive.

Not saying what your position is, is passive. Not looking for a way forward does not help solve or respect the other person's problem, so it is (to an extent) aggressive.

Assertiveness is exceptionally useful for:
* resisting unacceptable pressure from customers;
* saying 'no' when that is the only sensible answer;
* calming down angry or upset individuals.

Assertive people are not rude or pushy. They are able to say what they feel or think without giving offence.

A common problem when working from home is that you are under pressure from someone to deliver to an entirely unrealistic deadline. The client is being aggressive and it is hard to argue your point. There are only three options when this, or similarly difficult situations happen. Read them and decide which one would work best on you, if you were trying to get someone to do something for you. The options are:

1 Agree – even though what you agree to is either physically impossible, or means working without sleep for three nights.

2 Tell them not to be stupid – and lose their business, their respect or your job.

3 Say clearly, factually and honestly that:
* you understand their position;
* you have a position of your own;
* you think there is a way forward.

For example:
* 'I understand this is all urgent because your customer is pressing you. However, it simply isn't possible to do it all in the time. If I said I could I would only let you

down … and you don't want that to happen, do you?'
- 'If you tell me which parts of the job need doing first, I'm sure we can sort something out that I can do, and that keeps your schedule on track.'

Agreeing with your customer would get them out of your hair for the time being, but would lead to much greater problems later. Arguing doesn't solve the problem either. It just puts everyone's backs up and leaves them feeling foul for the rest of the day. Assertiveness is the only game in town.

# 6 USEFUL ADDRESSES, CONTACTS AND THINGS TO READ

## Useful Addresses

### Business and legal

**Association of British Chambers of Commerce**
Head Office, 9 Tufton Street, London SW1P 3QB.
Tel. 0171 222 1555.
A wide range of business support available to members, including library and database information, working in the UK and abroad.

**Business in the Community**
8 Stratton Street, London W1X 6AH.
Tel. 0171 629 1600.
An umbrella organisation for enterprise agencies; also encourages corporate support for charitable initiatives.
Scottish Business in the Community is at Romano House, 43 Station Road, Corstorphine, Edinburgh EH12 7AF.
Tel. 0131 334 9876.

**Business Link**
Tel. 0800 500 200 for details of your nearest Business Link office (Business Connect in Wales; Scottish Business Shops in Scotland; sometimes known as One Stop Shops); or see list in DTI's *A guide to help for small firms*.
UK-wide business support network, providing

211

independent advice and information. Backed by the DTI, this initiative is aimed at small firms and people setting up in business.

Here you can contact your local TEC, LEA and Chamber of Commerce all in one place. On-site Personal Business Advisers can give advice on your business plans, spot potential problems, and help you find the business support you need. Grant subsidised consultancy support may also be available through the Enterprise Initiative Consultancy Scheme.

**Citizens Advice Bureaux**

Middleton House, 115–123 Pentonville Road, London N1 9LZ. Tel. 0171 833 2181.

Local addresses are in the phone book. Give advice on a wide range of issues.

**Department of Employment Small Firms Division**

Dial 100 and ask for Freephone Enterprise. Information and counselling services for small businesses.

**Department of Trade and Industry (DTI)**

Ashdown House, 123 Victoria Street, London SW1E 6RB. Tel. 0171 510 0169 (publications) or 0171 215 5000 (general enquiries).

The DTI produces an excellent range of free booklets and information posters for people thinking of running their own business, including *A Guide to Help for Small Firms* (also available in large type, Braille and on audiotape) and *Setting up in Business*.

You can get a list of the DTI's *Small Firms Publications* from dti Small Firms Publications, Admail 528, London SW1W 8YT. Tel. 0171 510 0169.

**The Law Society**

For general enquiries or lists of lawyers in your area contact:

- The Law Society, 113 Chancery Lane, London WC2A 1PL. Tel. 0171 242 1222.
- The Law Society of Scotland, 26 Drumsheugh Gardens, Edinburgh EH3 7YR. Tel. 0131 226 7411.
- The Law Society of Northern Ireland, 98 Victoria Street, Belfast BT1 3J2. Tel. 01232 231614.

Telephone 0171 405 9075 for a copy of their *Lawyers for Business* leaflet and a list of members in your area. You can get free, initial legal consultation with a participating solicitor through The *Lawyers for your Business* scheme.

**Local Enterprise Companies (LECs)**

The Scottish version of Training and Enterprise Councils (see the telephone book).

**Local Enterprise Agencies (LEAs)**

List of local offices available from the dti, or, for your nearest LEA call:

- The National Federation of Enterprise Agencies. Tel. 0121 458 2000 extension 3955 (England and Wales).
- Scottish Enterprise. Tel. 0141 248 2700, or Highlands and Islands Enterprise Tel. 01463 234171.
- your local TEC, LEC or Job Centre.

In Northern Ireland, the Local Enterprise Development Unit (LEDU) provides the same service. Contact LEDU at LEDU House, Upper Galwally, Belfast, BT8 4TB. Tel. 01232 491031.

These agencies offer business advice to new businesses, including help with formulating business plans. A good source of links with the local business community. There are more than 400 LEAs across the UK. Most counselling services are free, but check first.

**The Patent Office**

Call 0645 500505 (local rate) for free literature, CD-ROM training pack and/or video; or 0171 438 4700 for general enquiries.

The Patent Office, Newport, Gwent, NP9 1RH

For Europe-wide Patents, and advice about designs, copyright and patents.

**The Chartered Institute of Patent Agents**

Staple Inn Buildings, High Holborn, London WC1V 7P. Tel. 0171 405 9450.

**Institute of Patentees and Inventors**

Triumph House, 189 Regent Street, London W1R 7WF. Tel. 0171 242 7812.

**Training and Enterprise Councils (TECs) or Local Enterprise Companies (LECs)in Scotland**

Refer to the telephone directory, directory enquiries, Local Enterprise Agencies or see the dti's *A guide to help for small firms*.

TECs offer training and small business support to meet the needs of small business owner–managers in the local community. Each TEC runs its own programme which will probably include:

- events to share information about the requirements, pros and cons of setting up your own business;
- subsidised (or even free) business consultancy and advice;
- training (open learning programmes and seminars) – includes specific skills (i.e. bookkeeping, marketing); general issues (i.e. setting up a business); and a range

of programmes for employees;
• Enterprise Allowance – a subsidy for starting your own business, especially for the registered unemployed.

# Specific interest groups
**British Coal Enterprise Ltd**
Edwinstowe House, Edwinstowe, Notts. NG21 9PR. Tel 01623 826833.
Gives help to new businesses setting up in former coal-mining areas.
**British Steel Industry Ltd**
Canterbury House, 2–6 Sydenham Road, Croydon CR9 2JL. Tel 0181 686 2311.
Gives help to new businesses setting up in former steel-working areas.
**European Information Centres**
Full list of EIC offices in the dti's *A guide to help for small firms*. Also, for advice from European Information Line. Tel. 0117 944 4888.
Information and advice about doing business in Europe, including legislative requirements.
**Livewire**
Hawthorne House, Forth Banks, Newcastle-upon-Tyne NE1 3SG. Tel. 0191 261 5584.
UK-wide networking group for young entrepreneurs starting up their own businesses. Also runs its own award scheme.
**New Ways to Work**
309 Upper Street, Islington, London N1 2TY. Tel. 0171 226 4026.
Information for employers on working from home.

**Rural Development Commission**
11 Cowley Street, London SW1P 3NB.
Tel 0171 276 6969.
Advice or contacts, and grants, if you are setting up business in a rural area (especially areas hit by unemployment in agriculture).
The following may also be able to help you acquire premises and source financial help if you are in Wales.
The Welsh Development Agency. Tel. 01345 775577 and The Development Board for Rural Wales. Tel. 01686 626965.

# Support groups
### National Group on Homeworking
Office 26, 30–38 Dock Street, Leeds, West Yorkshire LS10 1JF. Tel. 0113 245 4273.
Campaigning group for homeworkers producing information on homeworking and the homeworker's rights. (They do not provide information about employers/jobs).
### Rotary International of Great Britain and Ireland
Kinwarton Road, Alcester, Warwickshire B49 6BP. Tel. 01789 765411.
A fund-raising group attracting great support from local businesses. A good way to get to know other local business people.
### Round Tables (National Association of)
Marchesi House, Embassy Drive, Birmingham B15 1TP. Tel. 0121 456 4402.
Men only membership with associated ladies circle; a fund-raising group similar to Rotary.

**Women in Management**
64 Marryat Road, London SW19 5BN. Tel. 0181 944 6332.
A networking group for women managers.

**Own Base**
68 First Avenue, Bush Hill Park, Enfield EN1 1BN. Tel. 0181 363 0808.
Business and social network for anyone working from home. Newsletter, events, discount schemes and members directory.

**Telecottaging Association**
Wren Telecottage, Stoneleigh Park, Warwickshire CV8 2RR. Tel. 01453 834874.
See Telecommunications section.

**Federation of Small Business**
32 Orchard Road, Lytham St Annes, Lancs FY8 1NY. Tel. 01253 720911.

**Institute of Directors**
116 Pall Mall, London SW1Y 5ED. Tel. 0171 839 1233.
Membership is for directors of companies, proposed by another member. Useful networking group, with monthly newsletter, courses and seminars, and information service. Publications include *Directors' Liabilities* and *Guidelines for Directors*.

## Organisations
**Inland Revenue**
Comprehensive range of leaflets explaining every aspect of tax and savings you may come up against. For a complete list of available leaflets ask for Catalogue of Leaflets and Books (IR List). Contact your local Tax

Enquiry Centre or Inland Revenue office (address in your phone book).

**Customs & Excise**
General Enquiries – contact the Central Office in Southend. Tel. 01702 348944. For details of VAT registration, contact your local Customs & Excise Office (in your phone book).

**Contributions Agency**
For details about National Insurance contributions (including a starter pack) contact your local Contributions Agency (in your phone book), or Freephone enquiries 0800 393539.

**Employment Office, Job Centre and Careers Centre**
For advice on employment matters, and recruitment.

**Institute of Chartered Accountants**
The Institute of Chartered Accountants in England and Wales, Gloucester House, 399 Silbury Boulevard, Central Milton Keynes, MK9 2HL. Tel. 01908 248250.

**International Association of Book-keepers**
44 London Road, Sevenoaks, Kent TN13 1AS. Tel. 01732 458080.

# Company registration

For details of how to register a company, contact Companies House.

For England and Wales:
Companies House, Crown Way, Cardiff, CF4 3UZ. Tel. 01222 380801.

For Scotland:
Companies House, 37 Castle Terrace, Edinburgh EH1 2EB. Tel. 0131 535 5800.

For N. Ireland:
IDB House, 64 Chichester Street, Belfast BT1 4JX.
Tel. 01232 234488.
For details of existing registered companies contact:
Business Names Register, Somerset House, Temple
Street, Birmingham B2 5DN. Tel. 0121 643 0227.

## Co-operative Development Agencies, etc.
In England, contact:
The Industrial Common Ownership Movement.
Tel. 01132 461738.
In Scotland, contact:
The Scottish Co-operative Development Co. Ltd.
Tel. 0141 554 3797.
In Wales:
The Wales Co-operative Centre. Tel. 01222 554955.
In Northern Ireland, contact:
The Northern Ireland Co-operative Development Agency.
Tel. 01232 232755.

... and finally, if it all seems to be going horribly wrong:
**The Bankruptcy Association**
4 Johnson Close, Abraham Heights, Lancaster LA1 5EV.
Tel. 01482 658701.
Advice and support for anyone who is or fears they are
about to go bankrupt.

## Business Information Services
**British Library – Lloyds Bank Business line**
Up-to-date information about businesses and markets
(from directors' names to trade associations). Initial

enquiries free of charge (except cost of phone call).

Also, keep an eye on publications such as *The Economist* and *Financial Times*. They often publish surveys of specific industry and business sectors, which are useful for keeping in touch with developments, especially if you work as a contractor or consultant for larger businesses.

**The Telecottage Association**

WREN Telecottage, Stoneleigh Park, Warwickshire CV8 2RR. Tel. 01203 696986. E-mail 100114.2366@compuserve.com

Produce bi-monthly magazine, and fact sheets on topics including teleworking, setting up a telecottage, e-mail, and teleworking and disability.

# Grant finding

Department of Trade and Industry (DTI)

The Enterprise Investment Scheme is an informal source of financial and business support via a 'business angel' (usually a private individual) in return for an equity stake. Contact the DTI for further information.

**Local TECs and LECs and LEAs (or via Business Link)**

For advice contact your local office or:

The National Federation of Enterprise Agencies

Tel. 0121 458 2000 extension 3955 (England and Wales).

Scottish Enterprise. Tel. 0141 248 2700.

**Lloyds Bank Grantfinding Service**

Information database to help you discover if you are eligible for government and other grants. Available at discounted fee to Lloyds Bank customers.

**Princes Youth Business Trust**
Head Office 18 Park Square East, London NW1 4LH.
Tel. 0171 543 1234.
Also The Prince's Scottish Youth Business Trust, 6th
Floor, 53 Bothwell Street, Glasgow G2 6TS. Tel. 0141
248 4999.
Registered charity giving advice, and assistance with
business plans and possible loans or grants for young
people (under 29, or 30 if disabled), hoping to start their
own business. Special programme available to help
young offenders and ex-offenders.

... and finally:
Ask your local bank, Citizen's Advice Bureau or solicitor
(if you have one); they may know of local grant sources
for which local businesses alone are eligible.
*The Directory of Social Change*
24    Stephenson    Way,    London    NW1    2DP.
Tel. 0171 209 5151.
Publishes a range of guides listing grant giving trusts
across the UK. Guides include:
*The Guide to Local Trusts*
David Casson and Karina Holly, Directory of Social
Change.
A series of regional guides for the Midlands, North,
South and London (revised annually).
*A Guide to Grants for Individuals in Need*
John Smyth and Kate Wallace, Directory of Social
Change.

## Franchising

**Lloyds Bank franchise database**
Database of potential franchises around the UK. Contact your local branch for details.
**British Franchise Association**
Newtown Road, Henley on Thames, Oxon RG9 1HG. Tel. 01491 578049/50.
For information about taking on a franchise, the contracts you need to make, etc..

## Marketing

**Advertising Standards Authority**
2–16 Torrington Place, London WC1E 7HW. Tel. 0171 580 5555.
**Communications, Advertising and Marketing (CAM) Foundation**
Abford House, 15 Wilton Road, London SW1 0PR. Tel. 0171 828 7506.
**MOPS**
16 Tooks Court, London EC4A 1LB. Tel. 0171 405 6806. For information about mail-order advertising and regulations for national newspapers.
**Mail Order Traders Association of Great Britain (MOTA)**
100 Old Hall Street, Liverpool L3 9TD. Tel. 0151 2274181.
**The Office of Fair Trading (OFT)**
Field House, 15–25 Bream's Buildings, London EC4A 1PR. Tel. 0171 242 2858.

# Health
## Physiotherapy
Association of Chartered Physiotherapists in Occupational Health
14 Bedford Row, London WC1R 4ED. Tel. 0171 242 1941.
## The Back Store
330 King Street, Hammersmith, London W6 0RR. Tel. 0181 741 5022.
Specialist range of ergonomically designed office furniture, back supports and other related products. Mail order (except furniture) across UK.
## Health & Safety Executive
Information Centre, Broad Lane, Sheffield S3 7HQ. Tel. 0114 289 2345. Free enquiry line 0114 289 2345, and a range of advisory leaflets available.
Alternatively contact local offices, via the telephone directory.
## RSI Association
Chapel House, 152 High Street, Yiewsley, West Drayton, Middx UB7 7BE. Tel. 01895 431134.
For fact-file on Repetitive Strain Injury (RSI), with useful addresses and information, send an A4 stamped SAE (to cover a 100g pack).

*Personal problems*
## Relate Marriage Guidance
See your local phone book.
## British Association for Counselling
1 Regent Place, Rugby, Warwickshire CV21 2PJ. Tel. 01788 578328.

*Childcare and voluntary carers support*

**National Council for One-Parent Families**
255 Kentish Town Road, London NW5 2LX.
Tel. 0171 267 1361.
Support and advice for lone parents.

**Pre-School Learning Alliance**
61–63 King's Cross Road, London WC1X 9LL.
Tel. 0171 833 0991.

**Professional Association of Nursery Nurses**
2 St James' Court, Friar Gate, Derby DE1 1BT.
Tel. 01332 343029.

**National Child-Minding Association**
8 Masons Hill, Bromley, Kent BR2 9EY.
Tel. 0181 464 6164.
A membership group for child-minders, but they can provide information, including how to get in touch with child-minders in your area.

**Carers National Association**
20–25 Glasshouse Yard, London EC1A 4JS.
Tel. 0171 490 8818.
Advice and support for people caring for relatives at home.

**Parents at Work**
5th Floor, 45 Beech Street, Barbican, London EC2P 2LX.
Support for working parents, including those with children who have special needs.

*Disability*

**Centre for Accessible Environments**
60 Gainsford Street, London SE1 2NY.
Specialist design information and where to find it.

**Royal Society for Disability and Rehabilitation**
25 Mortimer Street, London W1N 8AB.
Wide range of publications, including leaflets on living and working space design.

## Office security and insurance
**Association of British Insurers**
51 Gresham Street, London EC2V 7HNQ.
Publishes list of all registered members.
**County Council (Fire Authority)**
See your local phone book
**Crime Prevention Officers**
Offer expert advice (free of charge) on making your home secure. Contact your local police station.
**Fire Protection Association**
140 Aldersgate, London EC1A 4HX.
Information leaflets on how to prevent and (if necessary) put out fires.
**Royal Society for the Prevention of Accidents (ROSPA)**
Canon House, The Priory Queensway, Birmingham, B4 6BS.
For up-to-date information on the latest safety regulations and legislation.

## Planning your office
**Royal Institute of British Architects**
66 Portland Place, London W1N 4AD.
Publishes full list of members.
**Ergonomics Society**
Devonshire House, Devonshire Square, Loughborough

Leics LE11 3DW. Tel. 01509 234904.
For information and useful addresses.

**Federation of Master Builders**
Gordon Fisher House, 14–15 Great James Street, London WC1N 3DP.
Organisation admits only experienced builders as members. Ask for local office to get a list of members in your area.

**Local Authority Planning Department**
See your local phone book.

**National Association of Plumbing, Heating and Mechanical Services**
Ensign House, Ensign Business Centre, Westwood Way, Coventry CV4 8JA.
Publishes a full list of members.

**Trading Standards Department**
See your local phone book.
Provide civil advice on consumer goods and your rights. Contact your local authority for the nearest department.

## Environmental Information

**Department of the Environment**
2 Marsham Street, London SW1P 3EB. Tel. 0171276 7700.

**Ecological Design Association**
20 High Street, Stroud, Glos. GL5 1AS.

**Friends of the Earth**
26–28 Underwood Street, London N1 7JQ. Tel. 0171 490 1555.
Provide leaflets on running an environmentally conscious home, including lists of suppliers.

**Scottish Ecological Design Association**
15 Rutland Square, Edinburgh EH1 2BE.
**Women's Environmental Network**
287 City Road, London EC1V 1LA.
Tel. 0171 490 2511.
**Waste Watch at the NCVO**
26 Bedford Square, London WC1B 3HU.
Publishes a range of information on recycling initiatives, including a national *Directory of Recycling Centres*.


# General reading

## Setting up and running a business
*Running a Home-Based Business*
Dianne Baker, Kogan Page 1994
*Office Organiser*
Louise Bostock Lang, Collins Pocket Reference, HarperCollins 1995
A complete guide to running an office, from ordering stationery to chairing a meeting.
*Making Serious Money from Home*
Sharon Maxwell-Magnus, Pan 1996
Includes interesting section on 20 ideas for making money from home with details of professional associations, etc..
*The New Guide to Working from Home*
Sue Read, Headline 1992
*50 Businesses to Start from Home*
Mel Lewis, Piatkus 1994
Snapshots of 50 very different careers that you can

pursue from home. Good for ideas if you don't know what to do!


# Looking after yourself

*Working well at home*
Christine Ingham, Thorsons 1995
Has a particular focus on the impact that working at home may have on you, your home life and personal well-being.

*Working Alone: Surviving and Thriving*
Mike Woods and Jackie Whitehead (in association with Diana Lamplugh and The Suzy Lamplugh Trust), Institute of Management/Pitman 1993
Focuses on personal safety when working alone.

*Publications by the Health & Safety Executive*, HSE Information Centre, Broad Lane, Sheffield, S3 7HQ (some free):
• You Can Do It
• Health and Safety at Work – the Act Outlined
• Health and Safety at Work – Advice to Employers
• 101 Tips to a Safer Business
• Report that Accident
• Essentials of Health and Safety at Work
• COSHH: A brief guide for employers
• 5 Steps to Risk Assessment

*Health and Employment*
A booklet by The Advisory, Conciliation and Arbitration Service (ACAS).

## Company guides

*A Guide to Working from Home*
British Telecom (free from BT; Tel. 0800 800878).
One of several easy-to-read BT booklets on working from home.
*Small Business Guide*
Lloyds Bank, Penguin
Details on the financial issues you need to think about when setting up and running your own business. Available free of charge to account holders, or for £16 from branches of Lloyds.

## Magazines

*Enterprise Magazine* (monthly)
Entrepreneur Magazines Ltd, Haland House, 66 York Road, Weybridge, Surrey KT13 9DY
*Home Business* (monthly)
Merlin Publications Ltd, 14 Hove Business Centre, Fonthill Road, Hove BN3 6HA
*Home Run* (approx. 10 issues per year, subscription only)
Cribau Mill, Llanfair Discoed, Chepstow, Gwent NP6 6RD. Tel. 01291 641222.
*Teleworker Magazine* (bi-monthly, subscription only)
Telecottaging Association, Wren Telecottage, Stoneleigh Park, Warwickshire, CV8 2RR. Tel. 01453 834874.
Up-to-date information on the latest training and technology.

## Tax matters

*Why you need a Chartered Accountant*
Institute of Chartered Accountants in England and Wales,

PO Box 433, Chartered Accountants Hall, Moorgate Place, London EC2P 2BJ. Tel. 0171 920 8100.
*Debt – a Survival Guide*
HMSO; The Office of Fair Trading
*Employing People: a Handbook for Small Firms*
ACAS; Telephone 01455 852225 to order a copy.
*Notes for guidance on business names and business ownership*
Companies Registration Office. Available from Companies House (see address below).
Each year, many organisations publish tax guides. Copies are often available from libraries, and publicised in the broadsheet newspapers.

# Telecommunications
*Teleworking*
Alistair Reed, Blackwell 1994
All you want to know if you're thinking about teleworking.
**BT Helpline.** Telephone 0800 800 860 or 0800 800 152 for their Teleworking guide, or other information about services and equipment BT can provide for homeworkers.
**Mercury Communications Information Hotline** 0500 500 020. For information about business lines, equipment and services.
At the time of writing, Mercury are particularly keen to break into the teleworking market and produce a range of helpful leaflets.

## Franchising

*An Introduction to Franchising*
dti Small Firms Publications, Admail 528, London SW1W 8YT.
For anyone thinking of becoming self-employed by buying a franchise.

## Marketing

*Successful PR in a week*
Claire Austin, Institute of Management/Pitman, 1992
*Successful marketing in a week*
E. Davies and B.J. Davies. Institute of Management/Pitman, 1992
*Advertising: What it is and how to do it*
Roderick White, McGraw-Hill 1993

## Directories

Listings of media publications and broadcasting contacts are available in larger reference libraries. A good way to check editorial and advertising copy dates. They include:
*The Media Guide 1996*
Fourth Estate
For names and addresses of print publications, broadcasting organisations, government agencies, pressure groups, etc..
*PR Planner*
Media Information Limited, Hale House, 290–6 Green Lanes, London N13 5TP.
*The Blue Book of British Broadcasting*
Tellex Monitors Limited, 47 Gray's Inn Road, London WC1X 8PR.

## Industry newspapers

Usually available on subscription only, but libraries may have copies. They include: *Campaign, PR Week, Media Week and Marketing Week*.

## Organising yourself

*Office Organiser*
Louise Bostock Lang, Collins Pocket Reference, HarperCollins 1995
A complete guide to running an office, from ordering stationery to chairing a meeting.

## Taking care of yourself

*Putting Assertiveness to Work*
Steve Morris and Graham Willcocks, Pitman, 1996
*Successful Time Management in a Week*
Declan Treacy, Hodder Headline, 1993
*The Essential guide to pensions – a worker's handbook*
Sue Read, Pluto Press
*Pensions Management* (monthly)
Financial Times, No. 1 Southwark Bridge, London SE1 9HL.
Learning Material Service (has information on healthy eating).
The Open University, PO Box 188, Milton Keynes, MK7 6AA.
*Food should be fun*
The British Heart Foundation.
*The Relate Guide to Better Relationships*

Sarah Lsitvinoff, Vermillion 1992
*Successful Stress Management in a Week*
Cary Cooper and Alison Straw, Hodder Headline 1993

## Office security and insurance
Fire and Safety at work: a basic guide
HMSO.
*Working Alone: Surviving and Thriving*
Mike Woods and Jackie Whitehead (in association with
Diana Lamplugh and The Suzy Lamplugh Trust),
Institute of Management/Pitman 1993
Focuses on personal safety when working alone.

## Planning your office
A Step by Step Guide to Planning Permission for Small
Businesses (Planning Authority).
*The Conran Home Decorator: Better Lighting*
Jeremy Myerson, Conran Octopus 1986
Detailed guide to types, benefits and sources of every sort
of lighting imaginable.
*Bodyspace Anthropometry, Ergonomics and Design*
Stephen Pheasant, Taylor & Francis 1988
Explains all the principles.
*The Essential House Book: The Complete Source Book of
House Design*
Terence Conran, Conran Octopus 1994
Looks at how our homes work, and how to get the best
out of how we design our interiors. Full of ideas.

## Environmental Information
*Duty of Care*

Department of the Environment, DoE Publications and Despatch Centre, Black Horse Road, London SE99 6TT.

A leaflet explaining all your responsibilities, if your business produces waste.

*Environmental Helpline*

Freephone 0800 585794.

For advice on any environmental issues which you should be aware of, as well as advice on Government programmes and initiatives.

# INDEX

235